THE OLD REGIME POLICE BLOTTER II

Sodomites, Tribads & "Crimes Against Nature"

Early Modern True Crime

With notes, translations and an introduction
by Jim Chevallier

Chez Jim Books ◆ North Hollywood, CA

Published by:

Chez Jim Books

To contact the editor, e-mail: *jimchev@chezjim.com*

ISBN:1434819418

Table of Contents

ABOUT THIS COLLECTION

True crime stories have interested readers since at least the eighteenth century, when English readers devoured The Newgate Calendar, which provided both lurid and quotidian details on assorted criminal cases. In France, the closest equivalent was provided by various editions, full and abridged, of the *Causes Célèbres*, or "Celebrated Cases", which however a modern reader may find to be too much of a good thing – instead of the brief summaries and trial excerpts offered in the English work, these volumes typically provided lengthy chapters on each case. Also, the cases themselves were generally exceptional ones.

This collection represents an attempt to provide for pre-Revolutionary France something closer to the Newgate Calendar in both brevity and variety. It has been assembled and for the most part freshly translated from a variety of sources, primarily official reports and periodicals. The cases are presented, with some exceptions, in chronological order within broad categories. A brief overview of the applicable Old Regime law introduces each of the types of crime. Most of the material presented here has not previously been available in English, and so is available for the first time to researchers or casual readers with an interest in the subjects covered here but unable to read the original French. The stories here – drawn, with a few exceptions, from contemporary sources – are varied and revealing, whether the reader is interested in the legal questions involved, the glimpses of daily life or simply the human dramas in each case.

NOTES ON TRANSLATION

The translations here are for the most part literal. However, legal jargon in any language can make for rough going and eighteenth century French judicial language has quirks likely to slow the modern reader. Notably, many terms occur in pairs of synonyms: "He stated and declared"; "We asked and inquired"; etc. With a few exceptions for color or emphasis, these are reduced to a single term in English.

Certain words slightly shift meaning in context, even if the same word is used consistently in the original French. Notably, *commerce* can mean "trade", "business", "intercourse", etc. Given the sexual nature of much of this material, the nuance is sometimes meaningful but also sometimes misleading, and so is translated as most appropriate, with the sacrifice of an evident ambivalence in the French. *Sieur* most literally means "Sir", but given the distinction between those for whom it was simply a conventional form of address or reference and those who were in fact aristocrats, the period equivalent "Master" is most often used, with variations where rank suggests it.

Several judicial terms – notably *quidam* and *le nommé* – are translated as "individual" or even omitted entirely in some cases. Also, the standard interrogation formula was often recorded as a series of questions – "Asked if..." – , even when the questioner was making a statement. In most cases this (admittedly confusing) construction has been retained to give a sense of the original.

The word *parlement* (very literally, a "speaking") is sometimes translated as "parliament". However the French institution was largely a judicial one – very approximately like the Supreme Court – and that distinction is best maintained by retaining the French term.

Most of the textiles mentioned were known in English by their French names and so are untranslated.

Spelling and punctuation in the originals is often inconsistent and has for the most part been retained as is. Orthographically alert readers should know that some key changes in French spelling occurred just in the earlier part of the eighteenth century, notably replacing certain letters with accents; for example, in the same trial record (for Deschauffours) "Saint Cosme" sometimes appears as the more modern "Saint-Côme" and "Châtelet" is also encountered as the more archaic "Chastelet".

The word *chirugien* is translated literally as "surgeon", but anyone new to the period should know that a surgeon for a long time was far below a doctor in status (closer, in fact, to a barber at one point). Those cited here might be regarded as somewhere between an EMS worker and a doctor in their level of skill.

Some amounts are given in *livres*. This very literally means "pounds", but is left untranslated, since the latter term becomes confusing when the same narrative includes English currency.

Finally, while personal and street names are not typically translated, in some cases here their meaning, if not directly related to the subject at hand, at least has resonance to a reader of French and so the French term is accompanied by a translation.

SODOMY

UNDER THE OLD REGIME, SODOMY, in common parlance, referred to sex between men. Legally however the term covered a range of actions from masturbation to necrophilia:

Of Sodomy, & other Crimes against nature.

The *sin against nature*, is committed principally in three ways:

1: When one falls into the crime called *Softness*, a name given it by the Apostle *Epist. 1, cap. 6, n. 10*, & that the Latins called *Masturbatio*.

The second type is the *Sodomy* which is committed *exercet venerem cum masculo, aut cum muliere, sed non in vase debito*; or finally when a woman *nubit cum alia foemina*.

The third type is when a man, or a woman *exercet venerem cum animalibus brutis*.

S. I.

Of sodomy

2. Sodomy is of all indecencies the most abominable, & one which has always been punished by the most severe penalties...

Note the generous – and atypical – doses of Latin in such passages, indicating a subject too awful to inflict on anyone but an expert. Basically, the terms included masturbation, sex with a man, as with a woman, "not in the proper vessel", sex with animals and sex between women:

> 11. The crime of women who corrupt each other is regarded as a
> type of sodomy, *si venerum inter se exerceant ad exemplum
> masculi & foeminae*; & it merits the ultimate punishment..

Jousse expands on the issue of sex acts between heterosexuals:

> The penalty for the crime of sodomy applies not only against
> those *qui non habent cum masculo*, but also to those *qui
> accedunt ad mulierem praepostera venere.*... And this penalty
> applies equally to those who act this way with their own wives...
> But the woman who is known this way by her husband must not
> be punished by death; unless it is proven that she gave this action
> complete and free consent.

He adds a few other points:

1. A person could kill anyone who 'attacked' them in this way (while this might generally refer to some degree of coercion or violence, in one account from the Bastille, 'attack' seems to refer to a simple approach).

2. A wife could legally separate from a man "subject to this vice".

3. According to some, a simple 'attack', consummated or not, could be punished by death, though circumstances and age must be considered.

4. 'Weakness of age' could excuse one who has 'let himself by corrupted, especially if he was the victim of violence.

5. Neither the testimony of witnesses nor of experts was required as proof, presumptions and/or the testimony of one who claimed to have been attacked could suffice.

The above is from Volume IV, 118-122 of *Traité de la Justice Criminelle*. The rest of the article also covers bestiality and necrophilia.

The *Encyclopedie's* article on the subject includes this note:

> Clergymen, monks, before [*or* 'owing'] the example of chastity,
> of which they have made a solemn vow, must be judged with the
> greatest severity when they are found guilty of this crime; the
> least suspicion suffices to have them removed from any function
> or post which involves the education of youth.

Officially, the standard punishment was death by burning, and
Jousse cites several cases where this was applied. But the Bastille
archives record many cases where the outcome was far milder
(most at the start of the century). Ravaisson, writing in the 19th
century, gives one creditable explanation for this:

> In granting the honors of the B. to the miserable debauched
> individuals in question here, the police wanted to avoid the
> scandal caused by trials before the Tournelle, and by the flames
> of the stake at which the guilty were burnt alive; it sought as well
> to remove from the public curiosity the declarations of the
> accused against their accomplices, and so to preserve the honor
> of families. These are the real motives of the indulgence of the
> King for a vice which he regarded with the deepest disgust and
> regarding which his most cruel enemies were unable to cast the
> least shadow of a suspicion.

Ravaisson, *Archives de la Bastille*, 1702-1710, 2

(Despite his harsh opening words here, the nineteenth century
Ravaisson, as will be seen, looked askance at one "investigator"
of others' sexual behavior.)

Sodomy was sometimes treated much like prostitution: many
sodomites were sent to the Hospital; the "public" nature of an
offense was often cited; "corrupting" others was an aggravating
factor. Otherwise, clergymen were often sent to a diocese in the
provinces. Too, far from sharing the modern American opposition
to gays in the military, the Old Regime, with admirable
pragmatism, viewed many as perfectly serviceable cannon fodder
and more than one sodomite was sent off to a regiment.

Probably class and simple favoritism played their part as well.
Saint-Simon fulminates frequently against the Duke de Vendôme,

who seems to have been one of those blatant incompetents who nonetheless has the boss' ear – the boss, in this case, being Louis XIV, who took a long time to realize how disastrous a general Vendôme was. This was all the more inconceivable because:

> The most wonderful thing to whoever knew the King—so gallant to the ladies during a long part of his life, so devout the other, and often importunate to make others do as he did—was that the said King had always a singular horror of the inhabitants of the Cities of the Plain; and yet M. de Vendôme, though most odiously stained with that vice—so publicly that he treated it as an ordinary gallantry—never found his favour diminished on that account. The Court, Anet, the army, knew of these abominations. Valets and subaltern officers soon found the way to promotion. I have already mentioned how publicly he placed himself in the doctor's hands, and how basely the Court acted, imitating the King, who would never have pardoned a legitimate prince what he indulged so strangely in Vendôme.

> Duc de Saint-Simon, *The Memoirs of Louis XIV. And His Court and of The Regency*, Volume 5 (Translator not named)

The composer Jean-Baptiste Lully was close to Vendôme as well as others of a similar reputation such as the Chevalier de Lorraine and the Count de Fiesque, all associated too with the King's brother, "Monsieur". Lully himself had more than one narrow escape and certainly owed his impunity to both his talent and his relations. (Joseph Prunières, "La vie scandaleuse de Jean-Baptiste Lully", *Mercure de France,* May 1916; p, 77.)

A similar dynamic applied for many more obscure figures as well.

Finally, most of the cases here for which details are given involve elements, such as pimping or approaching schoolboys, beyond sodomy itself. While it may not be that two men living quietly together were completely safe, here, as in so much else in Old Regime law, discretion seems to have counted for a great deal:

> In his Memoires, the police lieutenant-general Lenoir estimated at 20,000 the number of Parisian sodomites in 1725, and Mouffle

d'Angerville reported that in 1780 a police commissioner had shown his friends "a large book in which were listed all the names of pederasts known to the police.' He claimed that Paris had at that time "as many as it had prostitutes; that is 40,000."

Michel Rey, "Les Sodomites Parisiens au XVIIIe siecle", unpublished maitrise d'historien, Université de Paris VIII-Vincennes (1979-80) from Kent Gerard, Gert Hekma, *The Pursuit of sodomy: male homosexuality in Renaissance and Enlightenment*, Routledge, 1989

If either of these figures were remotely accurate (making allowances for false denunciations), only a very small percentage seem to have been actively prosecuted. This is not to suggest that homosexuals felt unthreatened under the Old Regime, but possibly most felt no more insecure than under the sodomy laws of succeeding centuries.

For a general discussion of homosexuality during the Enlightenment, see the *Gay, Lesbian, Bisexual, Transgender & Queer Encyclopedia*:

http://www.glbtq.com/social-sciences/europe_enlightenment.html

Before the eighteenth century, probably the most famous sodomy case was that in 1661 of Jacques Chausson, called des Etangs and Jacques Paulmier, called Fabri. This case is given in some detail later here. Both men were burned – without the mercy of a preliminary strangulation – at the stake. Otherwise, Jousse gives the following examples of executions (along with some earlier cases). The gap between 1677 and 1726 may simply reflect his own selection, or it may be due to the 'tolerance' that applied in the early years of the eighteenth century. The fact that the trial transcript was sometimes burned with defendants suggests how horrible some considered the very subject; one of the few other cases where this was done involved bestiality.

Jousse gives no details on these cases, though more appears later here about the very famous case of Étienne-Benjamin Deschauffours:

By a... Decision of March 31, 1677, an individual of sixty, guilty of this crime, was condemned to be burned in the New Market of Paris, which was carried out the same day.

Another Decision of 1671, which condemns Antoine Bouquet to be burned alive with his trial for this crime.

Another Judgement, delivered to the sovereign by the Chatelet of Paris, May 24, 1726, which condemns Benjamin Deschauffours, for the same crime, which was carried out.

Another Decision of June 5, 1750, in consequence of which Bruneau Lenoir & Jean Diot, guilty of this crime, were burned in the place de Greve, the following Monday, July 6.

Jousse, IV:120

SODOMITES

THOUGH SODOMY STRICTLY SPEAKING could be practiced between women and heterosexual couples, the term "sodomite" referred only to men. The cases here by definition address those who came to the attention of the authorities. By the late seventeenth century, this usually (though not always) resulted from activities that went beyond sodomy per se, such as pimping and prostitution or abuse of children. Almost inevitably, too, those actually punished, even if others were mentioned, were from the less powerful strata of society – a fact that did not go unnoticed by the public.

These cases are documented not only in the usual judicial sources – largely the Archives of the Bastille and d'Argenson's reports as head of the Paris Police – but in an early twentieth century French work dedicated specifically to sodomy trials: Dr Ludovico Hernandez, *Les Procès de Sodomie aux XVIe, XVIIe et XVIIIe siècles. Publiés d'après les documents judiciaires conservés à la Bibliothèque nationale.* (The author's name is a pseudonym, used by Louis Perceau et Fernand Fleuret, but will be retained here, being the name on the printed volume.) Hernandez is, among other things, far less squeamish than Ravaisson, who frequently redacts names and specific acts.

Chausson and Fabri

This is one of the most famous sodomy cases before the eighteenth century. Note that "Fabri"'s family name varies in different accounts (the trial record gives it as "Paulmier".).

Saturday, December 4, 1661

> M. the Criminal Lieutenant and councilors assembled to judge the trial against Jacques Chausson, called des Etangs, Jacques Saunié, called Fabri, accused of sodomy, et foul impieties; Mauger, student at Montaigu, age eighteen, also accused, judged separately, to be taken to Saint-Lazare, there to be held six months, under good and sure guard, and other condemned parties to the sentences which follow: "The said Chausson and Pannié condemned to make honorable amends before Notre Dame, to be taken to the Grève to be attached to a stake, have their tongues torn out and burned alive with the trial record, all to be reduced to ashes, thrown to the wind, condemned to sixteen hundred livres in reparations, to the benefit, for half to the hospital, and the other half to the Hôtel-Dieu, eight hundred livres of reparations to the Châtelet. The remainder of their confiscated goods to go to the King, and so declared against several people of quality and others.

> By order of the 29th of this month, the sentence has been confirmed and executed the same day, the day after the Christmas holidays.

> Matthieu Marais, *Journal et mémoires de Mathieu Marais ...: sur la régence et le règne de Louis XV (1715-1737)*, Paris, 1864, III:65

Though (as was standard practice in such cases) the trial transcript was supposed to be burned with the accused, modern researchers have found it in the French National library in a manuscript numbered 10969:

> Trial proceedings of Jacques Chausson, called des Etangs, former customs agent, forty-two years old, charged with sodomy and murder of an adolescent, and convicted of having served as a

panderer to others. He was condemned to have his tongue cut out (for the charge of blasphemy) and to be burned alive (for the charge of sodomy and complicity in sodomy). The execution took place December 29, 1669.

Robert Challe, Jacques Popin, Frédéric Deloffre, *Journal du voyage des Indes Orientales*, April 1690, p. 460

But the official record gave only one version:

Take the case of Jacques Chausson and Jacques Pamière (known as "Fabri"). They were convicted in the attempted rape of a seventeen-year-old boy (in 1661) and wound up admitting to procuring much younger boys. They were condemned to have their tongues cut out and to be burnt alive, which was done on December 29, 1661. In theory, the sentence called for their "customers" (a marquis and a baron) to be prosecuted, but they never were. The iniquity of this obvious injustice revolted the people, and many vengeful stories were written, such as the Complainte de Chausson et Fabri.

Jean-Claude Guillebaud, Keith Torjoc, *The Tyranny of Pleasure*, 21

No tragedy was so great nor crime so horrible that Old Regime humorists did not satirize it. The following sonnet is from Claude Le Petit, who would be burned himself in the *place de Grève* for the crime of divine and human lèse majesté:

Friends, they have burned the unlucky Chausson,
This rascal so famous, with curly hair;
His virtue was immortalized by his death;
Never has one died so nobly.

He sang a sad song with a gay air
And put on without blanching the weighty smock,
And from the burning pyre
Watched death without fear or trembling.

In vain his confessor preached to him through the flames,
Crucifix in hand, to think about his Soul;
Stretched out below the stake, when the fire had brought him down,

The swine turned towards Heaven his foul rump;
And, to show at the last how he had lived,
He showed everyone, the wretch, his ass.

Hernandez, who quotes this as well as the trial transcipt which follows, also provides these lines from the collection *Recueil de chansons pour servir à l'histoire anecdote, depuis 1600 jusque et compris 1664* (Bibl. nat., ms. fr. 15127):

I am the poor boy
Named Chausson,
Named Chausson
And if I was roasted

In the prime of life,
It was for love of a page

Of the prince of Conty.

If everyone was burned
Who did what they did,
Who did what they did,

Very soon, alas!

Several lords of France,
Great important prelates,

Would suffer death.

Let us pray then in this place

The mother of God,
the mother of God
And her noble son Jesus,
That all cocks grow,
That cunts shrink,
To no more be fucked.

(This is not the only such satire to portray female genitalia as frank adversaries.)

In 1674, when Lully had a fireworks display in front of his house and it went awry, one of the resulting bits of wit again referenced Chausson:

> Excuse, Messieurs, Baptiste's
> Giving you so sad and sorry a fire,
> And serving you poorly for your half-louis;
> The trial of Chausson goes on; if it ends
> He will give you another on the Grève,
> Which will please you more.

Prunières, 79

The transcript itself makes less entertaining reading. Not only were the two defendants rapists and kidnappers, but their insouciance at being caught in mid-rape suggests, at the least, a self-destructive obliviousness. It appears too that, whatever the law, they expected more consensual sodomy to go unpunished: "He found the said Jacques Chausson carnally coupled with Jacques Paulmier; that having wanted to point out to the said Chausson how great a crime he had just committed, the said Chausson told him that he should tell no one and that it was up to him to enjoy the same pleasure." And in fact this witness said nothing until the rape led to their arrest:

CRIMINAL TRIAL TRANSCRIPT OF JACQUES
CHAUSSON, CALLED DES ETANGS, AND JACQUES
PAULMIER, CALLED FABRY, ACCUSED OF THE CRIME
OF SODOMY, AND HAVING HAD THE SAID CRIME
COMMITTED

December 29, 1661

In the year 1661, Tuesday the twelfth day of August, appeared before us, Jean Baptiste des Molets, Commissioner at the Châtelet of Paris, Germain des Valons, Squire, lord of Duchesne, Lieutenant in the regiment of Montrevel, and Aymard de Bellesair, Squire, lord of Tremblay, who told us they were bringing complaint for the injury done to Octave Julien des

Valons, seventeen, minor son of the said Germain des Valons, lord of Duchesne, whom Octave Julien des Valons introduced fifteen days ago to the home of a certain Jacques Chausson, rue Saint Antoine, near the Vieille Rue du Temple, and that this morning, around ten thirty, a woman named Chrétienne Le Laboureur, working during the day, came to the home of the said Aymard de Bellezair, to warn him that the said Octave Jullien des Valons, his nephew was being attacked [*literally, 'assassinated'*] in the house on the rue Saint Antoine; that at the instant the said Bellezair have followed the said woman, went into a room in the said house, where having climbed to the second apartment, accompanied by valets, he effectively found the said Octave Jullien des Valons, all bloody, and struggling with several individuals, among whom was the said Jacques Chausson, called Des Estangs; that having pulled away by force the said Des Valons, his nephew, he went to find the above named Germain des Valons de Duchesne, his father, to come register the present complaint and verbal request; the said complainants added that they wish to pursue the said complaint, and asked for a certified copy, which we have presently given them; so signed: Germain Desvalons, sir de Duchesne, Lieutenant in the regiment of Monsieur the Count de Montrevel, and Aymard de Bellezair, Squire, lord du Tremblay, stipulants for Octave Jullien Des Valons, Squire, their son and nephew, the said request dated Monday the eighteenth day of the present month of August, whose sense is that the said Jacques Chausson, called Des Etangs, be declared for the injury and violence done Tuesday the twelfth of the said month to the said Octave Jullien Des Valons, mistreatment done to him and which he proposes to prove, as also that which the said Des Estangs wanted to force the said Des Valons to suffer carnal knowledge and habitation and against nature of an individual dressed in a red suit with golden braids, who was locked in his room;

Seen also by the above mentioned Lieutenant Criminal the complaint made at the home of master Des Molets, commissioner assigned for the police to the quarter of Saint Jean's Cemetery, the said day the twelfth of august, by the supplicants;

The statement by the said sir Commissioner Des Molets, the same day and the report and examination made in his presence by Grégoire Aubry, sworn Surgeon received at Saint Cosme, of the state and situation of the said Octave Jullien Des Valons;

We, Lieutenant Criminal in the Provosty of Paris, order that the said Jacques Chausson, called Des Estangs, living on the rue Saint Antoine, be taken and bodily apprehended, and taken prisoner to the prisons of the grand Châtelet, to be interrogated by us, and so ordered as proper; and for this command Raoul Rifflart, officer of sir the Lieutenant Criminal of the Short Robe, to execute the present order, and to take with him whatever number of men of his Company he considers appropriate, given for us this day Tuesday, nineteenth day of August.

First interrogations

Today the twenty-first day of August, was led and brought before us, an individual dressed in *gris de maure* cloth, the said individual currently prisoner in the prisons of the grand Châtelet, which individual we interrogated and questioned in the following way:

Asked his name, answered that he was named Jacques Chausson called Des Estangs.

Asked his profession and calling, responded that he had formerly been an agent at the King's tax collectors, but that, for two and a half years, he was no longer employed, and was obliged to live from writings and copies that he did for this or that person who wanted to employ him.

Asked his age, answered that he had turned forty three and a half on the twenty-fifth of the last month.

Asked about what led to the violence committed against the individual Octave Jullien Des Valons, Tuesday the twelfth day of the present month, answered that the said Des Valons, who came sometimes to his place, having boasted that he had a Rose marked on his buttock, he asked him to see it; that the said Des Valons having refused, but that he, Chausson, having bet a crown that he would see it despite him, started trying to unbutton his trousers, upon which the said Des Valons gave him a blow of his fist, but that the said Des Valons, feeling the weaker, started at once crying he was being murdered, and that someone was trying to rape him.

Asked who was the said individual dressed in red cloth, with golden braids on his suit, answered that he did not know him.

Questioned and threatened, should he not say the name of the individual which was known very well, and which he must no doubt know, to be put in prison, and in the case of a longer resistance, to have him put to the question, answered that the individual indicated above was called Jacques Paulmier, called Fabry.

After which requests and interrogations, the said Jacques Chausson was returned to prison by our order.

Done the day and year above.

On the request presented to Monsieur the Provost of Paris, Saturday the twenty third day of the present month of August, the King's Prosecutor joined to it: the said Request having for effect that following the criminal trial of Jacques Chausson, and following the testimony and declarations of the said accused the twenty first of the present month, Jacques Paulmier, accused of having wanted to rape and carnally know the said Octave Jullien Des Valons, be taken and declared under arrest; the conclusions of my lord the King's Prosecutor favoring the said order; we, Lieutenant Criminal, order that Raoul Rifflart, Officer, to take and apprehend the said Jacques Paulmier, called Fabry, to then take him to the prisons of the grand Châtelet of Paris, for the said accused to be questioned by us and this duly ordered, this day Tuesday twenty sixth day of the month of August.

Today Wednesday, the twenty-seventh day of the month of August, was led and brought before us an individual dressed in red cloth, with golden braids on his suit, currently prisoner in the prisons of the grand Chatelet of this city, whom we have interrogated and questioned in the manner and fashion which follow:

Asked his name, answered that he was named Jacques Paulmier, called Fabry.

Asked his profession, answered that he was currently an agent at his Majesty's general tax authority.

Asked his age, answered that he was thirty six.

Asked if he knew Jacques Chausson, called Des Estangs, answered yes, that they had been customs agents together, and that since this time they had seen each other a great deal.

Asked what had led to the violence committed by him against Octave Jullien Des Valons, Tuesday the twelfth day of the present month, answered that, during the conversation, the said Jacques Chausson had said that a man has no more strength, and is greatly hampered when the button of his pants is undone, upon which which the said Des Valons answered that he bet he could fight, and push even if the button of his pants was undone; upon which the said Chausson had bet a *pistolle* not, and the said Des Valons having undone the button of his pants, took a cane as if to use it for a sword, and instead of striking a blow, struck across the face Chaussons, who told him he was an oaf; following which the said Des Valons wanted to strike him with his cane, which the said Chausson held back with his hand, and was about to strike with his fist in the face Des Valons, who, feeling his weakness, cried out he was being murdered, and even that someone wanted to rape him.

After which interrogation, the said Jacques Paulmier, called Fabry, was taken by our order back to the grand Châtelet.

First witnesses

Today Friday, the twenty-ninth day of the month of August, appeared before us an individual dressed in cinnamon-colored cloth, who told us that he came to obey our order dated yesterday, which individual we questioned and interrogated as follows:

Asked his name, answered he was named Octave Jullien Des Valons, Squire, son of Germain des Valons, squire, lord of Duchesne and of the deceased Louise Angelique Du Vesien, his wife.

Asked his age, answered that he had turned eighteen this last March.

Asked about the argument he had, Tuesday the twelfth day of last August, with Jacques Chausson and Jacques Paulmier, in the second apartment of a house located on the rue saint Antoine, near the vieille rue du temple, answered that knowing the said Chausson, and having been taken to his place by the young man called Le Sueur, he finally came to his place the said day the twelfth of August, and that the said Paulmier had told the said Chausson in speaking to him of Des Valons: "Here's a cute little blonde!" upon which the said Chausson answered: "I think him a pretty enough boy to offer you his services"; to which Des Valons having replied that he hoped he was useful for something, the said Chausson spoke and said that the service they were asking of him would cost him nothing, and that the said master Paulmier was for his part obliging enough to return him the same when he wanted; that he Des Valons, having had the misfortune to reply that he did not ask more than to be able to fulfill for his part the desire he had to oblige the said Paulmier, the said Chausson came forward and having kissed him at the same time had undone the button of his pants, then the said Paulmier started trying to know him carnally, and then commit with him the crime of sodomy, which having felt, he started to cry out, and fought, so that an old woman, working by the day at the home of master Petit, hosier, principal tenant of the said house, came running, and that he told her to go to the house of sir Du Tremblay, his uncle, who lives in the neighborhood, vieille rue de Temple, at the corner of the rue de Bercy, and that a moment later the said sir Bellezair Du Tremblay came with his valets, and took him from the hands of the said Chausson and Paulmier.

After the said interrogation, the said Octave Jullien Des Valons withdrew.

Upon the request of the King's Prosecutor of this city of Paris, we Lieutenant criminal, have ordered several individuals of both sexes to appear in person next Saturday the eighteenth day of the present month of October, failing which the said individuals will be subject to extraordinary pursuits; with which order we have charged the said Raoul Rifflart, police officer from the company of sir Lieutenant Criminal of the short robe. Given by us today Thursday the sixteenth day of October.

Today Saturday the eighteenth day of the month of October appeared before us in person before us the witnesses named below, who, after having sworn the standard oath to speak the pure and entire truth have declared as follows:

The first witness, who has said he is named Marc Antoine Petit, wholesale hosier in Paris, and living on the great rue Saint Antoine, parish of saint Gervais, and principal tenant of a house facing the said street, near that of the Temple; who has declared that since the eighth day of last April he has rented the second apartment of the said house from Jacques Chausson, he has never heard any noise or disturbance, and that he has never seen any woman, girl, or other than many young men; that in truth, it was about three months ago that a woman came to yell at the said Chausson, and reproach him with having kidnapped her nephew, that she was going to complain at the Commissioner's; but that the said Chausson told him that the young man that this woman complained had been kidnapped was in truth her nephew, but that he was also his, Chausson's, cousin, that knowing the bad behavior and treatment she made him suffer, he had put him in school in the provinces; and finally the said Petit, first witness, added that he had been quite astonished by the disturbance and scandal at the said Chausson's place Tuesday the twelfth day of last August, thinking him incapable of ill doing.

The second witness, who said she was named Chrestienne Le Laboureur, working by the day at the home of sir Marc Antoine Petit, declared that Tuesday the twelfth day of the month of last August, around ten thirty in the morning, she heard a great noise and disturbance in the house of the second at the front, occupied by sir Jacques Chausson, and that being mounted and having opened the door, which had the key in it, she saw Octave Jullien Des Valons, his pants down, all bloody, and crying he was being murdered and that someone wanted to force him and to know him sodomitically, and that the said sir Des Valons had asked her to go to the house of sir Du Tremblay, his uncle, who lived on the vieille rue du Temple, to tell him come as fast as he could, which she did.

The third witness, who said he was named Joseph Henry Le Noir, declared that he had long known Jacques Chausson, he went one day to his place, when he lived on the rue des Noyers, near the rue des Anglois, with a linen merchant, and that some days before he came to occupy the apartment of the rue Saint Antoine, he found the said Jacques Chausson carnally coupled with Jacques Paulmier; that having wanted to point out to the said Chausson how great a crime he had just committed, the said Chausson told him that he should tell no one and that it was up to him to enjoy the same pleasure, and that besides he would be more careful in the future not to leave his key in the door in order not to be interrupted; that the said Paulmier then tried hard to get him to let himself be known carnally, which obliged him Le Noir, the current witness, to tell him that if he did not let him leave he would denounce them and at the same time have them punished for their crime, and then left this house.

The fourth witness, who said he was named Joseph Picard, called la Fleur, servant of monsieur the Count de Kesly, declared that being in the service of the said Jacques Chausson, at the time that he lived on the rue des Noyers, towards the fifteenth of last January the said Chausson arrived one evening with a very handsome young man, dressed in a mouse-grey suit, which young man he told to go to bed, and having no bed to give him, he would have him sleep in his, and that all night he heard the young man cry out and complain, upon which he having asked the said Chausson about the tears and cries of the said young man, the said Chausson had answered that the young man was from a good family, but that, unfortunately, finding himself a bastard, had been shamefully driven away by his brothers, who did not want to share their father's wealth with him, and that the uncle of the said young man, and brother of his mother, had taken this young man in, which uncle, having been obliged to come to Paris, and not wanting to appear to protect the young boy, had asked Chausson to house him secretly, until he returned to his home; that two or three days after, an old man arrived, magnificently dressed in a suit of blue velvet, embroidered on all the seams, which man the said Chausson told him was the young man's uncle; the said Picard adding that this man came every day to visit the said young man, that then the said Chausson closed the door, and that one heard the said young man cry and weep; that not knowing what all this could mean, he had followed the said man one day who passed for the uncle of the young man, and had seen him go into a great house on the rue de Vaugirard, in the saint Germain suburb, near the [convent of] the filles Religieuses du Calvaire, and that having inquired to the servants of the said great house, he had learned that the said man who had just gone in was the Master of the house and that it was Monsieur the Marquis de Bellay.

After the said questions and interrogations the said witnesses maintaining their said depositions and declarations, have declared that they are true and sincere; and have signed: Marc Antoine Petit, Joseph Picard called la Fleur, and so summoned the said Chrétienne Le Laboureur who declared she did not know how to sign. Done by us the day and year as above.

In the year 1661, Saturday the 25th day of October, were brought before us Jacques Chausson and Jacques Palmier, presently prisoners in the prisons of the Grand Châtelet, and also appeared those named above, Jean Baptiste Des Molets, commisioner at the Châtelet of Paris, agent for the police of the Saint Antoine district, Germain des Valons, Aymard de Bellezair, Octave Julien Des Vallons, seventeen years old. Raoul Rifflart, police officer, Grégoire Aubry, sworn surgeon received at saint Cosme, Marc Antoine Petit, Chrétienne Le Laboureur, Joseph Henry Le Noir et Joseph Picard called la Fleur, all witnesses in the presence of whom the acts, statements and statutes were read, which above name witnesses and accusers have declared and sworn to their prior testimony, true and sincere depositions, declaring that they maintained them, and signed the present statement. Done before us the above mentioned judge the day and year as above.

Toussaint Le Mouleur

Today wednesday the fifth day of November appeared an individual dressed in black etamine who declared to us she was named Aubertine Rivet, widow of Augustin Le Mouleur, when alive a Master pork butcher in Paris, the said widow complainant asking justice for the violence and kidnapping committed by Jacques Chausson and Jacques Paulmier against Toussaint Le Mouleur, her and the said Augustin Le Mouleur's son, kidnapped with violence by the said Des Estangs and Fabry over four months ago, which kidnapping the said Rivet had reported to the Commissioner Regnard Laisné Sunday the sixth of last July, accompanied by several witnesses, which complaint the said complainant brought us and showed us the copy signed by the Commissioner the sense of which follows.

In the year 1661, today Sunday the sixth day of July, appeared before us, Pierre Regnard, King's Counselor, Inquiring Commissioner acting of the Saint Eustahce district in Paris, Albertine Rivet, widow of Augustin Le Mouleur, when alive Master Pork Butcher in Paris, the said widow is complainant and asking justice for the kidnapping and violence committed on the person of Toussaint Le Mouleur, her son, and of the said Augustin Le Mouleur, by the said Jacques Chausson and Jacuqes Paulmier, which Des Estangs is said to have since several days attracted to his home the said Toussaint Le Mouleur, age fourteen, and finally held him in his house on the rue Saint Antoine, where the said Toussaint Le Mouleur is said to have been locked up until today Sunday the sixth of July, that the said widow Le Mouleur learned from the present witnesses whose names follow that the said Fabry came around eleven o'clock by coach to the house of the said Des Estangs, and also is said to have brought the said Toussaint Le Mouleur in the said carriage into a house on the rue des saint Pères, near the rue de Bourbon, from which he came out shortly after without the said Le Mouleur, who is said to have stayed in the said house; to which violence and kidnapping Pierre Hardy, called Sans Soucy, coachmen of the above-mentioned coach, also bore witness, and certifies that he took the said Fabry and Le Mouleur from the said house on the rue saint Antoine to the rue des saint Pères, in the saint Germain suburb [*today part of Paris*]; and the woman named Angélique Thérèse Quinet, daughter of Robert Quinet, Cloth Merchant, also testified that she had seen the said Des

Estang go in Friday the fourth of the present month, and that living in the same building as the said Des Estangs, she heard the said Le Mouleur who wept and cried that he did not want to leave his mother and go with Monsieur the Baron de Bellefore, rich and great lord though he was. Which is why we, the above named Commissioner, have, at the request of the said Rivet, prepared the current statement, of which we have delivered the current copy to be used as necessary. Done the day and year as above by us, the said Commissioner, so signed: Regnard.

After which reading the said Aubertine Rivet said that having learned that the said Jacques Chausson and Jacques Paulmier had been arrested, she asks that we give her justice for the said violence and kidnapping, in which demand she persists. Done the day and the year as above.

Second interrogations

Today Thursday, the thirteenth day of November, were brought into our presence Jacques Chausson and Jacques Paulmier, to whom was read the statement and request of Aubertine Rivet, as well as that of the complaint prepared by sir Regnard, after which we asked the said Chausson and Paulmier, accused, if they could respond to the said complaints.

Which Jacques Chausson answered that the said facts were false and slanderous.

Interrogated and threatened with torture if he chose not to respond, answered that he was ready to respond to each accusation.

Asked who was the lord to whom he had delivered Le Mouleur, answered that it was Monsieur the Baron de Bellefore.

Asked if the said sir Baron de Bellefore still had the said Le Mouleur, answered that he had learned that the said Toussaint Le Mouleur was deceased, since he the accused had been imprisoned.

Asked who was the young boy he had provided to the Marquis de... the fifteenth of last January, or thereabouts, according to the deposition of Jospeh Picard called La Fleur, servant of the Comte de Kerly, answered that this young man went to the country with the said Marquis du Bellay and so well worked his way into the good graces of his master, that he was made his first personal valet, and that besides the said young man was called Richard de La Monnerie, son of Jean de la Monnerie, chandler, living on the rue des vieilles Etuves, Saint Eustache Paris.

Asked if he had committed any other acts, answered no.

Asked if he had been paid by the said Marquis de Bellay to deliver to him the said Richard de la Monnerie, and by the Baron de Bellefore to deliver to him the said Toussaint Le Mouleur, answered that the Marquis de Bellay gave him fifty gold louis, and forty francs for the cost of food, and that the said Baron de

Bellefore gave him a present of a gold watch and of a gold tobacco holder which he sold together for seventy-eight gold louis.

In continuing the interrogation, we questioned the said Jacques Paulmier in the following way:

Asked what he had received from the said Baron de Bellefore, to whom he had delivered Toussaint Le Mouleur, answered that the said Baron had given him nothing, and that he had never been interested in taking money, that he had left everything to the said Jacques Chausson, which Chausson had promised to deliver him for a price the above named Octave Jullien Des Valons, whom he had seen several times at his place.

Asked if he had committed the said crime of sodomy with some others, answered that he had committed it with the said Chausson, and at the same time had suffered his carnal acquaintance, and he had also committed the said crime with a certain Doralier, officer in the Piedmont Regiment, who was killed in Flanders in the month of July 1659.

The sentence

Note that one of the harsher parts of the sentence that follows, the cutting out of the tongue, was not for sodomy but rather for the "blasphemies and impieties" mentioned; in 1766, the young Chevalier de la Barre would be given a similar sentence on that basis alone.

Sentence of Monsieur the Provost of Paris, or Monsieur his Lieutenant Criminal, of Tuesday the twenty-fifth of November 1671.

Seen by Monsieur the Provost of Paris or Monsieur his Lieutenant Criminal in the said City, Provosty and Viscounty, the criminal trial regarding Jacques Chausson, called Des Estangs, and Jacques Paulmier, called Fabry, defendants accused of having committed sodomy and crimes against nature, and generally all the pieces, circumstances and dependencies of the said trial; Given as well the conclusions of the King's Prosecutor at the Paris Châtelet;

We have found the said Jacques Chausson, called Des Estangs, and Jacques Paulmier, called Fabry, prisoners in the prisons of the Châtelet, guilty of having committed sodomy and crimes against nature, in reparation of which great crime they are condemned to make honorable amends naked in a smock, a rope around their neck, before the Church of Notre Dame of Paris, and being in their tumbrels, and head bare on their knees, and each holding in their hands a burning candle of yellow wax of two pounds, they will say and declare in high and intelligible voice that wickedly, maliciously and unhappily they have proffered the blasphemies and impieties mentioned in the trial, for which they repent, and ask pardon of God, the King and Justice. This done, they will be taken to the place of the Greve each to be attached to a stake and have his tongue cut out and then their bodies burnt and reduced to ashes, which ashes will be thrown into the Seine River. Further we declare that all and each of the goods belonging to the said Jacques Chausson and Jacques Paulmier will be acquired and confiscated to the appropriate person, upon which will nonetheless be levied the sum of sixteen hundred livres parisis as a fine, half applicable to the General

Hospital, and the other half to the Grand Hotel Dieu of Paris, and also the sum of eight hundred livres parisis as a fine for the King, in case the confiscation not be to the profit of the said lord King.

We further order that pursuit, upon request, be made by the diligence of the King's prosecutor, against the Marquis de Bellay and the Baron de Bellefore, accused of having kidnapped Richard de La Monnerie and Toussaint Le Mouleur, and with whom they have committed the act of sodomy and further still against the said Richard de la Monnerie. Given in Paris, by us Lieutenant Criminal, today Tuesday the twenty-fifth day of the month of November sixteen hundred seventy one.

In the year sixteen hundred seventy one, today Wednesday the twenty-fifthe day of November, were brought by Raoul Rifflart, police officer, Jacques Chausson and Jacques Paulmier, who told us that for the causes and means which they will lay out in the right time and place, they are appealing a sentence handed down against them by the Provost of Paris or his Lieutenant Criminal, on the twenty fifth of the current month. Done by me, concierge and guard of the prison and conciergerie of the Palace, the day and year as above.

Hernandez here provides the text of an interrogation that was part of the (typically standard) appeal to the Paris Parlement, the same day it confirmed the sentence, noting that "the ms. 10969 of the National Library does not reproduce this piece; it is at the National Archives, cote X 2 a= 1027 = 29 déc. 1661. M. Frédéric Lachévre has reproduced it in *the Oeuvres Libertines de Claude Le Petit*, Paris, 1918". Note that in the appeal Chausson claimed to be living off his means; this was probably no more than a way to avoid admitting living off prostitution. Otherwise, the appeal references numerous cases that do not appear in the preceding record, which may mean part of the former is missing or simply that other incidents had been mentioned but (unusually) not recorded:

December XXIX 1661.M. le président de Mesme, M. le président Le Coigneux, MM. Ferrand R., Doujat, Menardeau, Le Conte, Catinat, Petau, Le Clerc, Tronçon, Fayet, Bizet, Saint-Martin, Barillon, Brodeau, De La Garde.

Jacques Chausson, called des Estangs, 26 years old, living off his means and son of a linen merchant, bourgeois of Paris, declared that he bore arms in the Veilville regiment, has stayed at the house of his brother-in-law on the rue de Seine in the saint Germain suburb and in the rue des Boucheries.

Asked if [*that is, told*] he is accused of impiety and prostitution of young boys and committing the sin of sodomy and getting others to commit it and for this purpose trying to carry away young boys who came to his place several times with other people.

Said that only his friends came.

Asked if the witnesses with whom he had been confronted had maintained [*their declarations*].

Said that these are false testimonies which have been gathered, that he never sent his boy to the college of Montegu asking after a young schoolboy, did not give him a double pistol coin, that his lackey was called La Selle ["*The Saddle*"], whom he caught stealing, and that he did not know Du Val.

Asked what acquaintance he had with Godefroy.

Said that he did not know him at all.

Asked if he sang impious songs.

Said no.

Asked what acquaintance he had with Fabry.

Said that he has never seen him more than 3 or 4 times.

Asked if it was he who had brought Vignon to him.

[*Hernandez: "One will note the difference between these declarations and those of other interrogations at Chatelet. Further, there is question of facts and people which do not seem to be addressed by the Chatelet trial."*]

Said that no, that he was at the linen room of the college of Clermont.

Asked if he had not sent bottles of Spanish wine to Vignon.

Said no, that he did not know the little Marivaux, that he had has never had venereal disease.

Jacques Paulmier, called Fabry, 28 years old, served the lord of Montanegre, served the lord of Passage, was with an English gentleman.
Asked if it was in this country that he committed the sin of sodomy.

Said that he knows nothing about that.

Asked what acquaintance he had with Des Estangs.

Said that he met him at the Luxembourg [*gardens*] and found him sick and asked him what was the matter, he did not know him before that.

Asked if he had been to the Vincennes woods with a page and at St-Maur.

Said that he knows nothing about that, that he knows no page of Madame's.

Asked if he gave oranges to a page.

[*Hernandez: "In the songs on Chausson, which we gave in the Forward, there is mention of a page of the Prince de Conti, called Fesnaut. Yet in all the trial this is the only mention of a page."*]

Says that he gave him an orange, having found him in his sister's shop, he never went more than once to the college of Clermont, with sir Capau and others.

Asked if he spoke impiety with each word.

Said no and that he had never been part of this bad life, he ate once with Des Estangs and slept there one night and never saw anyone sleeping there.

Asked if he had not corrupted a young boy coming out of the bath.

Said no, that he only returned the last week of Lent from England, that he had never heard anyone speak of Gaborry, that he did not urge him to go sleep at his place, he frequented Vau... and was called De Breure, and that the witnesses were paid.

Ferrand, R.

[The rapporteur, named below as "Augustin";
the "R" may be a mistranscription]

Hernandez precedes what follows with this note:

December 29, 1661, the Court of Parlement handed down its
definitive decision in this matter and confirmed the sentence of
the Lieutenant Criminal. Note that the sentence of the Lieutenant
Criminal is reproduced differently in this decision, in regard to
the following passage: "... and to have the tongue cut out and
then their bodies to be burned alive, with the transcript of their
trial, and reduced to cinders, these thrown to the wine.. And
further on: ... and the other half to the Hotel Dieu of this city of
Paris; eight hundred livres parisis for the reparations of the
Châtelet and the same sum for the King, in the event that..." The
decision seems to foresee that the sentence will be amended:
"Said that it has been well-judged, badly and without cause
appealed by the said Chausson and Paulmier, and will amend it."

Nonetheless, this note is found after the signatures:

Master Augustin Ferrand, rapporteur [*roughly*, reporter; *a
special judge*].

Monsieur the President de Mesme,

President of the Tournelle.

Noted that there was no *retentum* for the present decision, and
the said Jacques Chausson and Jacques Paulmier, called Fabry,
were burned and executed alive.

A *retentum* was quite simply a note in many sentences that the
condemned person was to be strangled before the actual
execution. It was a standard mercy as the eighteenth century
approached, added for sentences like burning or breaking on the
wheel, which otherwise inflicted prolonged suffering. The fact
that it was not added for these two defendants is significant.

Hernandez adds a sonnet after this, found in a different hand at
the end of the transcript in the ms. 10969 of the National Library,
but says that it is "only a variant" of a sonnet written by Des

Barreaux on Vigeon, a maitre d'hotel who was burnt alive in Paris for having had "relations" with chickens (!):

> How many tears, Chausson, your Death will cost me!
> How unhappy to be a in a Country
> Where one is obliged to f. women in the c.
> And noble appetites are condemned to death.
>
> Order, judges, girls to be healthy,
> And that their [large] C.... become smaller,
> Without ever bearing flowers [*that is, a certain venereal disease*] or monthly flows.
>
> B-ggers, who saw him perishing in the Grève,
> On a burning pyre, without daring to help,
> To satisfy your lustful passions.
>
> Instead of sadly singing a Salve,
> You should all have shaken the pike [*that is, masturbated*].
> The c-- would have put it out and you would have saved him.!

(Hernandez points out some technical lapses in the French original, suggesting it was imperfectly transcribed.)

The navy guard

The first mentions of this man are for disobedience to orders. It is not clear if they are related to the charge below. Note that once again the arrest was not prompted by simple homosexual behavior but by abuse of a younger partner.

SEIGNELAY TO M. DE LA REYNIE

Chambord, September 17, [1685?]

The King has been informed that M. de Blémonville, navy guard of the department of Toulon, has been convicted of having committed the crime of s.... with a boy of twelve to thirteen years., H. M. wants you to have the said guard arrested following the orders which you will find attached, and that you order Auzillon to carefully seek him out in Paris.

Ravaisson, *Archives of the Bastille*, 1675-1686 (273)

Jacobite and friends

This is, among other things, an unusual mention of a Jacobite (many of whom settled in France and some of whose descendants played key parts in French history) and includes a casual slur of the Irish. The question of class and family relations is in the forefront here, especially in the different dispositions of each man's case, as is the explicit desire not to try these cases publicly.

The reference to "an order of the King" is to a *lettre de cachet*, which here was requested, as often was true, to spare a family's reputation. Though Neel himself ended up in Vincennes, it is worth remarking the chilling note that he is to be sent to the Bastille "and forgotten there". This annotation confirms the worst popular fantasy of the Bastille as an abyss into which prisoners disappeared forever. While this was far from common, in rare cases, that is exactly what was intended.

> CORRUPTER OF YOUNG MEN - August 30, 1701. - I have for a long time known Neel as a libertine, and sir de la Guillaumie for a debauched person, but I did not think that their behavior had reached this excess of corruption which I have just discovered.
>
> Several young men of seventeen or eighteen... having obliged me to have houses watched where I was told they were seen, this research has left me no doubt that sir Neel had seduced them, and that after having used them in the most criminal way, for himself, he sold them to sir de la Guillaumie, his friend, and to some other scoundrels who have long conducted this foul traffic.
>
> Among them has been named to me sir du Mas de Saint-Venois, brother of the counselor of Parlement who has been so much spoken of, and I will try to come to a complete knowledge of this cabal of abomination which cannot be pursued with too much zeal.
>
> I have had sirs Neel and la Guillaumie arrested, but the third has escaped me; the two prisoners could not help but admit their crime, and the young men were found following directions they gave me.

I have known, since their imprisonment, that Neel is from Ireland and that his father died in the service of King James, who gives a small pension to his mother. He was himself an officer in the Albigeois regiment, but his debauchery got him kicked out and his mother solicited another employment for him.

He has often been accused of theft, and several commissioners have received complaints for it. He has even often been heard to say that he was Irish, and could not help stealing [!]. But his petty thefts could not support him, and his disorderly temperament could not stop at one vice; there is none that has not been familiar to him, even impiety.

Sir de la Guillaumie, though of a calmer nature, and of a more austere humor, is not of a less irregular conduct, but since he seems to have only attached himself to one type of excess, the public avowal he makes of it makes it that much more scandalous: you remember no doubt, that I had him imprisoned, last year, for having sung licentious songs under the windows of the college of the Jesuit fathers, and if, then, I had examined his behavior more closely, it would have been easy for me to convict him of the same crimes of which he has declared himself guilty, on this last occasion.

You know that it was no less inconvenient to deliver these three defendants to the rules of the ordinary procedure than to hide their disorder; thus I think that Neel deserves to be transferred to the Bastille, to be forgotten there; that it is a kindness to sir du Mas de Saint-Venois to exile him to Tulle for a few years. Regarding sir de la Guillaumie, monsieur the first president of Rouen, his brother-in-law, and his brother, counselor in Parlement, ask as a favor that he be locked up, by order of the King, in the house of the brothers of Charity at Charenton, and they promise to leave him there a long time.

René d'Argenson, *Rapports inédits du lieutenant de police René d'Argenson* (1697-1715), 72-74

Pontchartrain agreed in all cases, but had Neel sent to the Chateau of Vincennes (which, unlike the Bastille, still stands today, though it served a very similar purpose.)

Lebel

Again, a case involving lackeys and valets. Several individuals are mentioned here, but the story that emerges tends to center on Lebel (who may, given the dates here, have been denounced by Petit). His is the kind of arrest of a minor player that makes numerous more prominent persons nervous. Merely being mentioned in such a case would lead people to draw conclusions. Regarding the letter to Tallard, for instance, Ravaisson notes: "The duke of Saint-Simon said, with no other comment, that M. de Tallard did not get on well with his wife; one sees here the cause of their misunderstandings, and that the wife was not completely in the wrong." Pontchartrain's concern that Desforges be interrogated secretly grows directly from his concern for any families whose members may be mentioned.

Lebel's very dense deposition does indeed include names of people known from other sources as sodomites (not to mention some rather catty gossip). It should not be forgotten however that he probably thought it was in his best interest to provide as many names as possible.

Overall, this set of documents reads almost like a novel, with a broad sweep including both tragic and comic elements, an unusually comprehensive look at the "sodomite scene" of the period and elements of prostitution and child molestation mentioned alongside of enthusiastically consensual activity. It also (however fortuitously) benefits from the literary trick of leaving unexplained holes in the narrative, which in this case were probably due to the chaotic state of the files following the fall of the Bastille.

A few random notes:

• It is amusing to see how Petit's name incrementally grows across successive reports to "Petit de Boution de Coubertin".

- His father's being a "farmer" may refer to a tax farmer, rather than an agriculturalist.

- Lebel – who is described as very good-looking – has a name which translates, if a little archaically, to "the handsome one".

- Chaulot and Chanlot appear to be the same person; one version is obviously a transcription error.

- On the rather tasty sounding meat dishes eaten by Petit and his friends, Ravaisson says, "It was no doubt Lent; we will note as a moral detail that the commissioner seems to find the inobservation of the fast as grave a crime as that he is denouncing to the lieutenant of police."

- In regard to private imprisonment at the home of the police officer Aulmont (and his father), though this practice was already outlawed at this point, exceptions were permitted for certain types of cases. The discretion required here may have been one reason for initially holding Petit apart.

- The Bastille's Tower of the Well, at the northwest corner, looked out over a rear courtyard which included a small well. The Tower of the Chapel once held the old chapel, which was replaced by one on the other side.

- Junca's mention of a "pierced cage" is unusual, and seems to suggest some kind of barred enclosure within the cell itself. No other account of the Bastille seems to mention such a structure.

- Pontchartrain's mention of a "confrontation" refers to a standard stage in the normal (and extremely bureaucratic) procedure when the accused was confronted with his or her accusers. Its absence here is one indication of how separate this case was kept from the normal judicial system.

Complaint and arrests

PETIT [in April 5, 1702, out April 16 1704]; DESFORGES [April 19, 1702-July 27, 1702]; LEBEL [May 10, 1702-January 11, 1703]; LOUVART [May 12, 1702 (died there June 18)].

Debauchery

COMMISSIONER BIZOTON TO M. D'ARGENSON.

Martin and his wife, who maintain a furnished room on the rue de Seine, near the Galley, have come to inform me that for a month, they have rented a room to a young man, named Petit, of about 25-26 years of age, with a handsome face, who receives day and night and brings several young men with which, not only does he make a debauchery of meat and other things, but still more prostitutes himself to all the young men who come to find him in his bed, until 3 o'clock in the afternoon, when he gets up and gets dressed. Then goes out to the public games to find other company, whom he brings back to spend the night at his place; that last night, they were again six and ate there a loin of veal and a quarter of lamb; that they having noticed that their bed was all spoiled, and having complained of this to Petit, he threatened to have them killed if they mentioned that to anyone; that he was to leave his room tomorrow, and go lodge very near, above the Galley; that this young man is very criticized for his excesses, and that everywhere he has lodged, he has been put out because of his debauchery; that they have not been able to find out more about his region and his family, than that he was from Beauce, and proud of it; that he frequented a young man who says he has the honor of being your in-law or relation, but could not know the name. As this information seemed to me of great importance, relative to this foul debauchery, I thought myself obliged to inform you of it, in awaiting your orders which I will execute punctually.

March 19, 1702

I have just arrested, executing your orders, Petit de Boution, and taken him to M. Aulmont's. He told us he is a native of Chevreuse, son of a farmer, that he has been in Paris for four years. When I browsed through his papers which I found enclosed in a round trunk, it seemed to me that he had formerly been the personal valet of M. de Gadagne, and I found a sealed letter addressed to M. the count of Tallard, lieutenant general of the King's armies. All these letters are filled with discourse which prove, what is more, the abominable trade which he has long practiced, and yesterday he had a private supper with a man of good family who is highly suspected of this disorder; his papers have been returned to his trunk, locked, and the key in his possession, and the trunk in the hands of M. Aulmont. I believe if you are good enough to examine this man, you will learn frightful things on his trade.

March 22, 1702

Lebel is a good-looking lad, well made, formerly a lackey, and who at present passes himself off as a man of quality.

This man is in the worst debauchery, and it is a place where one sees enter every day young men with people of quality and even monks, who pass whole days in the greatest debauchery, and it is said that the sin of Sodom is committed there with complete freedom.

Note that this is now two memoirs given against this man regarding this debauchery, and that he was driven from the parish of Saint-Sulpice, and from there went to live behind the Capuchins, in a house very suited to this kind of debauchery.

PONTCHARTRAIN TO THE SAME

Versailles, April 5, 1702

You will find enclosed an order to put in the B. Petit de Boution, where you must interrogate him fully on his bad trade, and send me his interrogation with the documents found in his trunk, after which we will see if it is better to put him in Vincennes or some distant castle.

JOURNAL OF M. DU JUNCA

Sunday April 9, at 8 o'clock in the evening, M. Aulmont le jeune brought and delivered M. Petit de Boution de Coubertin, near Chevreuse, etc., who is suspected, and even accused of being a sodomite, the which has been detained more than 15 days at M. Aulmont's, whom I received upon his arrival, and had put in the first room, alone, in the Tower of the Well.

PONTCHARTRAIN TO M. D'ARGENSON

H.M. is quite willing to drive Desforges from Paris, as you suggest; but he must first be interrogated on the things of which he is accused. I am sending you for this purpose an order to have him taken to the B., where you will submit him secretly to an interrogation which you will send me, if you please, which being known only by you and the clerk, will cause no prejudice to the families which find themselves involved.

JOURNAL OF M. DE JUNCA

Monday April 24, at 8 o'clock in the morning, M. Aulmont le jeune brought and delivered M. Lelièvre, lord Desforges, claiming to be a gentleman and master clockmaker, etc., who is accused of having talked too much and made bad speeches in society, whom I have received and had put in the third room of the tower of the Chapel, in the pierced cage, well closed.

PONTCHARTRAIN TO M. D'ARGENSON

H. M. is willing to put in the hospital general Lebel and Louvart, but they must first be interrogated about the crimes of which they are accused. As there is no confrontation to be held, this will be a short procedure, and if you want to hide it entirely from public knowledge, you can send them to the B. for a few days.

JOURNAL OF M. De JUNCA.

Friday May 12, at 4 o'clock in the afternoon, M. de Savery, etc., brought in M. Dupressoir-Louvart, said to be the son of a wigmaker, dressed as a marquis, whom the governor has received, and had put in the first room of the tower of the Chapel, locked.

Sunday May 14, at 9 o'clock in the morning, M. de Savery brought in M. Lebel, being in the same affair as Dupressoir, there being one order for both, whom I had put in the fifth calotte [top] room of the Bertaudière, locked.

Lebel tells... all?

AUTOGRAPH MEMOIR OF M. D'ARGENSON, INITIALED
BY LEBEL

June 2, 1702

*NOTE: This seems to be a secret interrogation of the sort
requested by Pontchartrain for Desforges. Given the number of
names it mentions, his concern was justified. The note that it is
'autograph' seems to indicate that d'Argenson himself
documented the interrogation, which was extremely unusual,
unless it is merely a formality indicating that a clerk took notes
under his direction. But it seems likely that in the end he did not
even trust a clerk to hear what Lebel had to say.*

People with whom Lebel has committed the sin of sodomy.

He is 24 years old and a native of Paris. His father is a personal
valet of M. de Chaulot, secretary of commandments of the late
M. the Prince, and he studied at the college of the Jesuits until
the second level, after having been a choir boy at Saint-Sulpice,
for 3 years. Duplessis, notorious sodomite, who lodges near
Saint-Etienne des Grecs, and walks every day in the
Luxembourg garden to seduce young schoolboys there, was the
first to corrupt him, and it was in this same garden that he
listened to his foul propositions; he was then only 10 years old,
and from then on Duplessis had almost everyday a group of
young men whom he successively abused.

He furnished him to Coutel, who lives in the Palais-Royal, and
who is not only a sodomite, but impious.

Astier was from the same group; all three go to the Luxembourg
and in the billiard halls of the place Saint-Michel, almost every
evening, to have parties with young children, attract them to the
tavern or in their room, and there commit the worst
abominations.

As they have no means, and they live only on this scheming,
they deliver young men whom they have debauched to people
who pay them well, and they share the price.

The abbé of Villefort, who was in the B., and since driven from Paris for similar horrors, also knew him and furnished him to M. de Ch., discharged colonel, who gave him a gold louis, and then pretended he was his soldier; but his friends got him out of this. He knew several other people whose principal study was to corrupt youth and conduct an open traffic of them. Here are their names:

M. Leroux, who lives behind the church of the Madeleine, boasted of this in his presence; the former sends handsome lackeys to lords in the countryside, when asked, and arranges here the conditions of their engagements. Comtois, lemonade-vendor, who maintains his shop in the rue des Bons-Enfans, near the Palais-Royal; M. de Sancerre, de Montpellier, who lodges in the rue Dauphine, across from the hotel d'Anjou; M. de la Guillaumie, abandoned to all sorts of debaucheries, and shut up among the PP. [*Pères* - Fathers] of Charity of Charenton, by order of the King, at the request of his parents; Baptiste, who was in the service of M. de Vendôme, and has long abused his confidence, going so far as to boast that he furnished him young men, and that he was well paid for it; M. the abbé of Capistron, who seems to have been charged with the same task; M. the abbé de Larris, formerly in the Sainte-Genevieve quarter; the latter has an agreeable appearance and prostituted himself on his own; the abbé Lecomte, who was driven from the seminary of Saint-Magloire, is a native of Paris, and for a long time has made it his principal study to attract schoolboys to corrupt them; the abbé Dumoutier, good friend of the abbé Lecomte and in the same trade; the abbé Bruneau, who has several relatives in the robe [*the judiciary*]; the abbé Servien, and it is said that he has in the quarter of Saint-Paul a private house which he only uses for this purpose.

M. the duke of L. [*Jean-Francois Paul, duke de Lesdiguières, son-in-law of the Marshal de Duras*], who in August 1699, being accompanied by a person of distinction whom he [*Lebel*] did not know, asked him to come sup with them, although he had never spoken to him, which he did not agree to do.

He knows as well that the people of this abominable trade meet up at Chez Livry, lemonade-vendor of the place of Palais-Royal, but does not think Livry is involved in this.

Has heard said that the last ambassador of Portugal was this way, and that he had in his service a tall page name Louis, whom he had since made his gentleman, and who, after the departure of the ambassador had quite a brilliant carriage in Paris.

It was said then that the duke of Lesiguières loved this page and that he gave him a lot of money, and recalls that a ring of one hundred louis was spoken of.

The son of Alvarez [*then a famous diamond merchant*] and the abbé Bailly, son of the mistress of the president de Maisons, close friends; Robert or Gobert, closet valet at the duke d'Orleans'.

Suspected the young duke d'Estrées, of having this same leaning, and knows that he wanted to raise up a tall very good-looking lackey, whom he found in the church of the Jacobins, into his service, which caused talk in the evening at the Tuileries, as the most ridiculous thing possible.

Formerly Father Armant, of Paris, capuchin, was involved in these abominations. This was before he took orders, and now he lives an exemplary life. He lives in the convent of Saint-Honoré, and he was known in the life under the name of Ville-aux-Bois; he has for uncle M. Amoung, clerk of the great council, and he is about to be ordained a priest.

The respondent offers to uncover in this style the most secret intrigues of Paris, above all in regard to regents and tutors who corrupt the innocence of their schoolboys, and he only asks for all payment to be shut up in Saint-Lazare, on bread and water, while waiting to be considered worthy to take orders at Joyenval, which is a Premontain monastery, fulfilling the vow he has made. M. the bishop of Chartres is the abbot of this abbey, where he was about to be received, when he was arrested and brought to this castle.

"It is the despair"

This was far from the only suicide in the Bastille and only one due to these sorts of charges. This prisoner, like most who died in the Bastille, was buried at St. Paul's under a false name.

JOURNAL OF M. DU JUNCA

Sunday June 18, at 11 o'clock in the morning or thereabout, Dupressoir-Louvart, prisoner locked up alone, in the first room of the tower of the Chapel, with no appearance of sickness or madness, except for a venereal disease, which a despair led him to cut off all his noble parts, entirely removed and thrown by himself into the corner of his fireplace, and seeing that he would not die of this fast enough, and that the hour when he was to be brought his dinner approached, he took his same knife, and cut his throat all the way to the bone. A moment later, M. Lecuyer, captain of the doors, going in his room to bring him his dinner, found Dupressoir on his bed, dying, covered with blood. Having come at once to alert M. the governor, and ask M. Giraud, the confessor, who ran there at once; but having found him incapable of talking, he showed by signs, that he understood everything the confessor told him, and even had enough strength to lift himself up, and indicated that he wanted to write. He was at once brought what was necessary. Who then wrote on a piece of paper: I ask pardon of God with all my heart; it is the despair. He continued to show good signs of a repentant Christian until his death, which was at 8 o'clock in the afternoon. M. the governor having informed M. d'Argenson, he came the evening of the same day, alone, to be informed of this unfortunate event, and what was to be done, having found him dead; it was agreed that he would send the next day Monday, at 7 o'clock in the morning, the commissioner Bizoton, alone, to have the body examined, and a statement of the condition in which he found him, which he did in the presence of MM. Corbé, lieutenant of the company, of Rosarges, officer, of Reil, surgeon, & of R., turn-key [*possibly Ru, a kindly guard mentioned in many other connections*]. This procedure done in the morning, the priest of Saint-Paul came to remove Dupressoir-Louvart's body, which was buried under the name of Pierre Massuque, in the presence and care of La Coste, sergeant of the company, and of some soldiers - Monday June 19, 1702.

PONTCHARTRAIN TO M. DE SAINT-MARS [*the Bastille governor, or warden*]

June 19, 1702

I have received the letter which you have written me concerning Louvart, who fell into despair; the best way to prevent this sort of accident is to not leave the prisoners any knives or other things they can use to a bad purpose, and to visit and have them visited often; I understand by the word often, the morning, the evening, and 3 or 4 times a day, and even at night, those whom one might suspect.

Decades later, the journalist Simon-Henri Linguet, one of the Bastille's most famous prisoners, would complain bitterly of being deprived of sharp instruments. Stories such as this one explain why.

Loose ends

The outcomes for the figures in this case, several of whom were involved in prostitution or abuse of children, are probably more typical than in the better-known and spectacular cases that ended at the stake:

THE SAME [*Pontchartrain*] TO M. D'ARGENSON

Versailles, June 21, 1702

I have read to H. M. the interrogation which you have credited to Lebel; he wants you to fully investigate and in detail all the miseries and abominations of which he began to tell you, in promising to have him received in Saint-Lazare, as he wishes. Work then on this business incessantly, with no concern for whom he could name; you will judge better than anyone of what importance it is to look further into what concerns the regents and tutors who corrupt schoolboys.

Marly, July 1702.

When you have learned from Lebel the names of the young men he has indicated to you, take the trouble to send it to me and to await the orders of the King before having them arrested.

July 28, 1702

I am sending you the order to have Desforges put in the hospital; he will stay there 2 years, after which he will be driven from Paris.

JOURNAL OF M. DU JUNCA

Thursday August 3, at 10 o'clock in the morning, M. Aulmont the elder [*l'aîné* - the other is the younger, *lejeune*] came, etc., to take M. Lelièvre.

Desforges, gentleman, who worked on clocks and guns, who being detained here, has been transferred to the hospital general, to be held there until further orders from the King. - Accused of several foul acts.

Desforges was taken to Bicêtre.

PONTCHARTRAIN TO M. D'ARGENSON

Versailles, April 16, 1704

Petit de Boution is to be taken to the hospital, from where he can be sent to the Chartreux, if he finds some convent willing to receive him.

REPORTS OF M. D'ARGENSON

Lelièvre, sir Desforges, etc.

In 1702, he was at the B., for several months; he tried to corrupt young girls of 10, and it does not seem appropriate to release him yet.

In 1701, Lebel, his father, being head butler at the hotel of M. de Chanlot, secretary of commandments of M. the Prince, and this young man, perverse since childhood, after having studied in a college of this town, and given himself over to the foulest prostitutions, held at his home a school of abominations and sodomy; he is convicted of every disorder by his own confession; but after having been 9 months in the B., he has asked with insistence to be transferred into this house (Saint-Lazare), there to do a somewhat more voluntary penitence; nonetheless, his spirit still seems restless, which makes it to be feared that his conversion is still quite uncertain.

I have even learned that since he has been in Saint-Lazare, he has given new proofs of his perverted and corrupted inclinations, despite the protestations and oaths so often repeated which he has used to fool me. Thus, it is no longer as a favor that he must be left in this house, but by reason for justice and penitence.

Martin Petit, put in Bicêtre.

In 1704, he came from the B., and is a quite unworthy character; sodomy was the principal occupation of his youth, and when the prostitution of his person became useless, he prostituted others and made a revenue from it. Here he wants to be a chartreuse monk, there he wants to be a soldier, and he would be suited enough to it without the perverse habit of which he is possessed.

In 1705. I think even that one could give him to an officer in confidence, in forbidding him to let him come to Paris, where it is to be feared that the sight of his old comrades make him return to his old disorders.

Pontchartrain's note: Give him for a soldier in the regiment of Noailles.

May 31, 1706.

PONTCHARTRAIN TO M. D'ARGENSON

April 19, 1705

I am sending you the order to release Lebel from Saint-Lazare; see that he immediately goes to the employment M. du Tronchet wants to give him, his freedom being granted him only on that condition.

The file ends with a poignant, and, for Pontchartrain, unusually compassionate note:

THE SAME TO M. DE SAINT-MARS

November 28, 1706

You will see by the plea of Louvart's mother, the request she makes for a diamond and the things of the deceased; I do not doubt that you will return to her everything that belonged to him. Thus, I have told this woman to address herself to you and to justify to you that she is her son's heir; because if he had a wife or children, it would be more just to give them his things.

One thing he does not mention, and which was almost certainly not returned to her: her son's body, which lay under another name in the graveyard of St. Paul's.

The exile's return

D'Argenson does not say why this man was originally exiled from Paris, but the "shameful sodomy" of his youth would have been reason enough. Class and the accused's prospects of an income seem to be major considerations here.

ARREST OF A DEBAUCHEE. [June-July 1703] I have also had arrested sir de la Parizière, another exile who, after spending his youth in a shameful sodomy, prostituted young men or sent [them] along the promenades. The officer who took him into custody told me this morning, that he had told him frankly that having, back home, a very bad and very boring wife, he preferred staying in Paris, at the risk of being taken to Fort l'Evesque and that after some very incoherent speeches, he made others which showed clearly that his mind was disturbed. He has, he says, the principal lands of Poitou and of Touraine. Nonetheless his father's whole fortune consists in being the captain of the Guards of M. the duke of Roannez. Further, he has infinite claims against all the lords of the Court; he even has a considerable suit against madame de Maintenon and, despite his enemies' cabal, he will enjoy fifty thousand pounds of income, before May of next years.

Pontchartrain's note: "To the Hospital".

(127)

The priest on the quai

This case is most interesting for the vivid deposition which starts the file. For a sodomy case, it is unusually detailed, reading almost like fiction. It would be useful to know exactly whose testimony Aulmont le Jeune recorded here, since the statement portrays all the men as being more or less willing participants, as far as things went. Some possibilities are that:

- The priest himself (after a lengthy interrogation?) gave the full truth of each encounter

- The other men involved added their accounts to his, being careful to avoid any mention of their own sexual activity

- The other men told the complete truth, and had reasons other than sexual interest for seeing the priest again (free drinks?)

On the face of it, the fact that both saw him a second time hints at there being more to the story.

As mentioned earlier, Aulmont, like his father, seems to have kept prisoners in his house, a practice that was being limited at this time. (It probably lasted longer in England; readers of *Great Expectations* may remember Pip barely escaping such private imprisonment in his case for debt.)

The word '*brayette*' (now '*braguette*') can be understood from context, but would be easier to translate both before or after our period. Once it was a codpiece, now it is a zipper. In the eighteenth century, it was still sometimes translated as "codpiece" (Boyer says "bodpiece"), but this is a bit misleading, since French definitions often refer to it as a "slit". No translation for this seems more appropriate than the French word itself (which was sometimes used in English at the time).

CHABERT DE FAUXBONNE

[Entered the Bastille May 14, 1704, left July 5]

Debauchery

AULMONT LE JEUNE TO M. D'ARGENON

April 29, 1704. Abominable priest. Gillain being Monday, April 28, 3 o'clock in the afternoon, on the parapet of the quai Neuf [*later the quai Pelletier, going from the Notre Dame bridge to the place de Grève, now the Hotel de Ville*], at the end by the strand [*grève*], and watching individuals who were playing at ninepins at the bottom of the quai, where second-hand coal is sold, an individual with short hair, and dressed in a cassock and long coat, like a priest, leaned on the parapet, near Gillain, and struck up a conversation on the game. Then this individual asked Gillain, if he was from Paris, if he was married, and if he had children? To which he answered that he was Parisian, married for three years and with a child, the priest said, What, only one child after so long; what aren't you doing? And flattering Gillain, and asking him if he wanted to take him to his room, that he would pay a bottle, that they could drink together; to which Gillain responded that he did not have the time. Then this priest left him, and the next day, 29, at the same time, at 3 o'clock in the afternoon, the priest returned and attacked [*sic*] Gillain, who was still on the quai Neuf with some coal dealers, and the priest having asked to drink good beer, Gillain took him to his room, where they drank a pint of beer which the priest paid 18 deniers for, and then the priest proposed to Gillain that both get in his bed, and that he f.... him from behind, and at the same time took his parts out of his *brayette*, and wanted to put his hand on those of Gillain, who repulsed him, and said that he saw clearly what he wanted of him, but that he did not have time, that he had to go sell wood in the boats, but that he would come back some other day, when he had more time, and they left each other after finishing their beer, and the priest promised to come see him the next day or after.

Chabert, priest of the diocese of Dié, Thursday, May 8, around 6 in the afternoon, accosted, on the quai Neuf Simonnet, saying hello. M. Simmonet was surprised, answered him: I do not know you at all. Nonetheless Simmonet who wanted to know this priest better, took as true the answer given by this priest who replied that he knew Simonnet and that he had seen him on the rue Montorgueil; the ice broken, this priest asked Simonnet where he lived, and he answered him that he lived on the rue aux Fèves; this priest told him: Let's go to your room. Simonnet agreed, they went together to Simonnet's room, which is M. Aulmont's attic, where there was so far only one table. This priest told Simonnet: You amuse yourself sometimes with your friends, that [sic], do you want us to amuse ourselves together, and at the same time he took his parts out of his brayette. At which Simonnet pretending not to know what the priest wanted, said: I don't know, M. l'abbé, what you are trying to tell me. This priest answered: What? Don't you have fun sometimes? Simonnet answered him: Ah! I understand, M. the abbé, but I don't have time today, tomorrow we will see, and said to this priest: what is your name then, M. the abbé, and where do you live? This priest told him he lived on the rue du Sépulcre [later the rue de Dragon], at the place of Delaunay, an invalid, was called Fauxbonne, and said his mass at Saint-Eustache.

The next dame, Simmonet being in his room, this priest came at 4 o'clock in the afternoon, and having come in, he said again to Simonnet,: And so, how about today? But Simonnet using the pretext that a man neighboring his room could see them, told this abbé to come back at 6. The abbé left and came back at 6, but finding no one, left.

He made similar propositions to several people, who are: Gillain, boot scraper, whom he knew only under the name of Claude; a carpenter's helper living on the rue du Sépulcre, Deslandes, a wigmaker's boy, to whom he only paid compliments. He does not say mass at Saint-Eustache, as he said, but he has said it at La Charité. He does not have his letters of priesthood, he only has promises at the bottom of his certificates which are sealed; among these sealed papers, there is a rough draft of a complaint to the King against his bishop.

PONTCHARTRAIN TO M. D'ARGENSON

Versailles, May 14, 1704

Regarding the sodomite priest, Chabert de Fauxbonne, he cannot be shut up in the hospital too soon; I will send you the order for that which nonetheless you will not execute until you have interrogated him thoroughly on the facts of which you have knowledge, and to avoid the *chartre privée* [private prison], you can put him in the B. for a few days, in order to submit him to interrogation at your convenience.

JOURNAL OF M. JUNCA

Sunday May 18, at 8 o'clock in the morning, M. Aulmont le jeune, took Chabert de Fauxbonne, priest, being from the town of Dié, etc., having stayed under arrest eight days at Aulmont le jeune's place, is accused and convicted of sodomy, wicked priest, who has been put alone in a dungeon cell.

PONTCHARTRAIN TO M. D'ARGENSON

July 5, 1704

I am sending you an order to take from the B., Chabert de Fauxbonne, and send him to the Hospital for 6 months, from which he will not exit except to return to the diocese of Lyon, at which time I will write to M. the archbishop of Lyon to have his conduct watched...

JOURNAL DE M. DU JUNCA

Thursday July 10, at 3 o'clock in the afternoon, to give to M. Aulmont, two prisoners for transfer: M. de Chabert de Fauxbonne, priest, and la Chesneau, wife of a soldier of the guards, and they have been taken; the priest to Bicêtre, and the woman to the hospital general, which M. Aulmont took charge of.

REPORT OF D'ARGENSON

November 15, 1704.

Chabert, he is 30 years old, native of Valence in Dauphiné; is an abominable priest who has dishonored his vows by a public profession of sodomy, and that one may nonetheless, to unburden the hospital, send to his region, on condition that he retire to a seminary as directed by his bishop.

Pontchartrain's note: Good on these conditions and be informed of his conduct by the bishop.

PONTCHARTRAIN TO M. D'ARGENSON

Versailles, February 11, 1705

M. the bishop of Valence is not persuaded that Chabert, priest of his diocese, who was shut up in the hospital, is guilty of the crime of which he is accused; I am sending the orders to have him released and to oblige him at the same time to retire to the diocese of Valence; you may inform the bishop, who is currently in Paris.

THE SAME TO THE BISHOP OF VALENCE

February 11, 1705

Regarding what you have written me concerning Chabert, priest, the King agrees to his being released, on the condition nonetheless that he retires to your diocese, where it is more just that he be than in another, particularly under the eyes of a prelate as attentive as you are to the good morals of the clergy.

1702-1710 (213-216)

Disgraceful propositions

D'Argenson's gracious application here of his superior's "suggestion" was probably a tactful way of following orders. The fact that Pontchartrain forwarded an order to send the priest to the Hospital, then had second thoughts, suggests some behind the scenes intervention, or at least due, if delayed, consideration of the Church's authority.

DISGRACEFUL PRIEST. - [May 29, 1705?] I am to receive new information concerning the sodomite priest who calls himself the abbé de Rochefort, and to be given some other letters which he has written to a young wheelwright of Vaugirard, by whom he was charmed, as by the lackey he loves so strongly. The one and the other state that he has made them the most disgraceful propositions, but they do not admit to having accepted them.

Priests at Saint-Sulpice regard him, finally, as a monster of impiety, but since there is no question of a State crime the judicious consideration which you have done me the honor of suggesting persuades me that it would be enough to return him to the diocese of Mans, which is his, and to alert his bishop, so that he may observe his conduct; thus I will not execute the order which you have done me the honor of sending me for shutting him up in the Hospital, and will return it to you when you like.

Pontchartrain's annotation: "To M. the cardinal of Noailles, [for] his opinion".

D'Argenson, 127

The three lackeys

It may not be surprising that lackeys appear in this and other sodomy cases. One way for a man to spend a great deal of time alone with another man without causing talk would have been to keep him as a servant, and more than one lackey mentioned in this connection had been a personal valet.

Pontchartrain's remark that these men do not deserve "the honor of the Bastille" is a rare but clear indication of the fact that, as Paris prisons went, the Bastille's accommodations were considered superior.

Bertaut and Labrie appear to be the same person, in which case "La Brie" is probably a nickname indicating Bertaut was from the Brie region.

LANGLOIS, BERTAUT, ALEXANDRE

[entered February 21, left April 21, 1706]

Debauchery

PONTCHARTRAIN TO M. D'ARGENSON

February 24, 1706

I have informed the King of what you have written me
concerning the sodomite men in livery. H. M. considers it proper
to first put Langlois, Labrie and Alexandre in the B., in order that
you may interrogate them in depth as soon as possible and know
their abominable intrigues, the company they keep and the whole
mystery of iniquity of which you will send me a full account
with your advice on how to proceed, because you can clearly see
that such people do not deserve the honor of being in the B.

D'ARGENSON REPORTS

Langlois, put in Bicêtre April 25, 1706

He is 24 years old, from Paris. He was brought to the B. for sodomy; he was a partner in debauchery of Bertaut, also a lackey, and they held assemblies in taverns of the Saint-Antoine quarter, where they committed the worst abominations. Langlois was nicknamed in these assemblies M. the grand master, and Bertaut the mother of the novices. This one is in the hospital, by virtue of an order of the King, limited to one year, which is only to expire the 25th of April of next year, but it would be quite just, it seems to me, that a rascal of this sort only be set free on condition of joining the troops, where he will be in a state to serve well, if his courage matches his size.

Pontchartrain's note: Enroll him and be sure of whom he is given to.

Bertaut, same. He was taken to the B. for sodomy; he was partner in debauchery with Langlois, but this one was a little less guilty. His time is to finish in January, and he has enlisted in advance with M. Rancher, captain of the Enghien regiment, to whom he could be taken now, if the King agrees.

Pontchartrain's note: Free him, drive him from Paris.

Ravaisson, 1702-1710, XI:283-284

Corrupters of youth

This is one of the few cases here where it is entirely possible that the defendants were punished purely for their sexuality – if that is the "young men" in question were (as seems to be the case) actually men and not, as in several other cases, very young teens. Certainly, the punishments for all were quite far from the theoretical severity of the law.

Buranlure's role here is not clear, and only his association with the other defendants suggests that he might have been considered a sodomite (though the reluctance to name the reason for his detention is significant as well.)

Lecomte's promises to change are not unique; nor is the accusation of mixing impiety with sodomy.

Probably the most striking case here is that of Lamothe. The police's concern with the welfare of his creditors shows a surprising (and very pragmatic) sense of priorities.

D'Argenson to Pontchartrain

M. de Buranlure entered the 5th [of September 1714?]. M. the chancellor knows the motives of the detention of this prisoner, who complains loudly of a retention of urine and of a very painful colic. He says he has had several attacks since he has been in this castle; otherwise, he looks very well.

These last three prisoners are foul and corrupters of youth: the first, which is de la Mothe, is a merchant whom I have had the honor of suggesting to M. de Pontchartrain to send away for two or three months in the monastery of Charity of Charenton.

The other is Lecomte, who, though deacon of the diocese of Paris, has spent his time for several years in seducing young men and attracting them to disorderly behavior; he was shut away once in Saint-Lazare, and his detention was followed by his exile to the seminary of Evreux, where he claimed he was resolved to end his days; but he left almost immediately, and he has since

continued his seductions and his horrors with more license than
ever; thus I think no house is better suited to this Lecomte than the
hospital, and that he must be shut up there for a very long time.

Regarding Roger, he is a tonsured cleric of the diocese of
Angers, and so cited for his foul behavior by several people of
merit and virtue, that one cannot doubt that he has mixed impiety
with sodomy.

Ponchartrain to d'Argenson

August 21, 1715

Regarding Laisné, it seems that by his answers, and by what
Lemure said when he was confronted with him, that there was
more imprudence and facility in his conduct, and that he never
took part in the foul actions of those he frequented; this has
determined the King to grant him his freedom, and I am sending
you the order you need for this purpose. H. M. hopes,
nonetheless, that you will reprimand him severely for the people
he frequented, and let his conduct be closely watched, so that it
can be corrected if it is not absolutely regular in the future.

D'Argenson to Pontchartrain

September 25, 1715

You know that A. Roger, son of a master tapestry-weaver, was
put in the B. the 11th of last month, convicted of the most foul
debauchery; but his father having submitted in writing to watch
his conduct and teach him his trade, from which his past
debaucheries had so long turned him away, it seems he can be
freed.

You know that P. Delamothe, mercer in Paris, in the rue aux
Fers, was taken to the B. after having been convicted of the most
awful debauchery, but as his detention upsets his business
dealings completely, and could cause the entire ruin of his family
to the detriment of his creditors, of whom there are many, I think
it is appropriate to free him, on the assurance he has given of
being more careful in the future.

Malignac to Hérault

May 17, 1715

I have the honor of informing you that the abbé Le Comte who
has been locked up several times for sodomy in the hospital,
which he only left after being relegated by the King, is actually
in Paris, where it is said he continues his same life, and gets
drunk from morning to evening.

Ravaisson, 1711-1725, XIII:180-183

The Desfontaines case (guest-starring Voltaire)

It was not unusual in Old Regime France for people to hire pamphleteers to libel others. In one of the more famous bits of verbal venom from a period rich in it, a lord is said to have berated one such pamphleteer for his lies about him. The writer responded, "But my Lord, I need to live."

"I see no need for it," came the answer.

According to Voltaire, this story concerned the abbé Desfontaines, whose libels-for-hire had drawn the ire of the count d'Argenson. Certainly, unlike other defendants mentioned here, Desfontaines was well-known in the literary world:

> I have just tried reading *Gulliver* which I had already read, and that the translator, l'abbé Desfontaines, had even dedicated to me. I do not think there is anything more disagreeable. The conversation with the horses is the most forced, the most cold, the most fastidious invention one could have imagined.
>
> Mme Deffand to Horace Walpole, July 1780

La Harpe summed him up as follows:

> This abbé who had been a Jesuit himself, had wit and literary acquaintances; he was besides a mediocre writer, an impassioned critic and a weak translator.
>
> La Harpe, *Correspondance Littéraire*, Paris, 1801, I:338

What is more, if Voltaire is to be believed, he is depicted in one of the more famous pornographic works of the time:

> *Le Portier des Chartreux* is a book which is not of the most austere moral. One finds in it a portrait of the Abbé Desfontaines franker than anything to be found in Petronius.
>
> Voltaire, *Oeuvres Completes*, Paris, 1893, VII: note 225

Voltaire, however, is not always trustworthy, and he knew how to nurse a grudge: "Whether his hatred was justly or unjustly founded Voltaire was never known to forgive" (Henri Van Laun, *History of French literature*, 1877, III:70) .

He had particular reasons to dislike Desfontaines. In regard to Voltaire's role in the current case, and their subsequent quarrels, several sources say essentially the same thing:

> It was said that Desfontaines owed [Voltaire] nothing less than his life. It is certain that he got him out of Bicêtre, where this man had been locked up for foul crimes; and it is stated that, since this time, the abbé Desfontaines had written many libels against his benefactor.
>
> Voltaire, VII:note, 238

Voltaire's version does not differ substantially from more neutral accounts:

> I only knew the abbé Guyot Desfontaines because M. Thiriot brought him to my house in 1724, as a man who had been a Jesuit, and who, consequently, was a studious man; I received him with friendship, as I receive all those who cultivate letters. I was shocked at the end of fifteen days to receive a letter from him, dated from Bicêtre, where he had just been locked up. I learned that he had been put three months before in the Châtelet for the same crime of which he was accused, and that he was being formally tried. I was then fortunate enough to have several powerful friends... I raced to Fontainebleau, sick as I was, to throw myself at their feet; I pushed, I solicited in every direction; finally I obtained his relief and the interruption of a trial which was a matter of his life: I got him the permission to go to the country at the house of M. the president of Bernieres my friend. ....Do you know what he did? Wrote a pamphlet against me. He even showed it to M. Thiriot, who forced him to throw it in the fire; he asked my pardon in telling me the pamphlet was written a little before the date of Bicêtre. I had the weakness to pardon him, and this weakness earned me a mortal enemy...
>
> XX:260

(Any reader of French who would like to read an extensive follow-up to the above can see the "Memoir de Sieur Voltaire" which begins Volume 24 of the Hachette edition.)

It could not have helped that he seems to have influenced Fréron, whom Voltaire called "A worm born from Desfontaines' ass." (VII:216)

Attacking Voltaire was, in one sense, unwise. On the other hand, it did prolong many a non-entity's butterfly reputation, pinned to history by Voltaire's wit:

**Epigram on the Abbé Desfontaines
who spoke out against attraction**
(1738)

For antiphysical love
Whipped Desfontaines
Has, they say, spoken harshly
Of the Newtonian system.
He has taken completely backwards
the purest truth;
And his errors are always
Sins against nature.

The Abbé Desfontaines and the Chimneysweep

Told by the late M. de la Faye.
(1738)

A chimneysweep with a sunburnt face,
Iron in hand, the eyes covered with a blindfold,
Was sliding up a chimney,
When from Sodom an antique beadle,
Who for Love took this youngster
Climbed on back of his bent spine.
Love cried out: the neighborhood came running.
A statement was taken; and Desfontaines in heat
Is caged up in the walls of Bicêtre.
They tie him up, they strip him down.
A nervous hand took pleasure in putting the spurs
To the heavy butt of the sodomite priest.
Girls laughed, and the flayed acolyte

Cried out: "Monsieur, for God's sake, be touched;
Read please, my verse and my prose"
The spanker read; and suddenly, still angrier,
He doubled the renegade's dose,
Twenty strokes of the whip for his wicked sin,
And thirty more for the boredom he causes us.

VII:331-332

Side stitches

The Desfontaines case introduces the most notorious of a type no doubt found throughout such histories.

In Vidocq's dictionary of thieves' slang (*Voleurs, Physiologie de Leur Moeurs et Leur Langage* (1837)) he says that a "*Point de côté*" is an "enemy of pederasts" (27). Though Vidocq began his criminal career before the Revolution, he did not write about it until the nineteenth century, and so one can only guess which of the terms he recorded in 1837 were already in use under the Old Regime. But, as many are still used today, this one may have applied in our era.

The literal term today means two very different things: a minor injury due to jogging and in knitting, a rib stitch. To complicate matters, Vidocq says a 'point' was also slang for a franc, so the term may have meant nothing more than someone who got money on the side (as an informer).

For this context the most appropriate translation seems to be "side stitch", meaning a pain in the side, a concept which no doubt existed (with all its more vulgar variants) before jogging, and which has obvious application here. (It also rhymes nicely with "snitch", creating a kind of inadvertent cross-lingual rhyming slang.)

Around 1713, d'Argenson mentions a minor example of the genre, though he seemed to have been a good old fashioned informer, who may well have been in it for the money:

> DENOUNCER - I am assured that a certain de la Javière has given very good information against notorious sodomites who have been put in the Bastille or the Hospital. I therefore think that a compensation of one hundred pounds could not be put to better use.
>
> Pontchartrain responded: "Good. Once."

d'Argenson, 318

The Abbé Théru, on the other hand, seems to have been a kind of shadow Savanarola, determined to root out (sexual) transgression in all its forms. Though he only seems to be mentioned (twice) in connection with this case and briefly in that of Deschauffours, Ravaisson apparently knew (and did not like) far more about him than he set down:

> This abbé Théru is a terrible man; he gave himself the mission of
> tracking down debauchery of every sort and among every rank;
> the number of people he had locked up is amazing; his zeal
> seems to have been disinterested, never does he speak of money;
> it is he to the contrary that, on occasion sends his game to the
> lieutenant general of police's table.

Archives de la Bastille, 1709-1772, XII:n. 121

He earned himself the tiniest of footnotes in history by insinuating – in the fullest sense of the word – that Voltaire, who had defended Desfontaines, was gay. Though Voltaire did defend Desfontaines, he claimed (not quite convincingly) not to know him well. Ravaisson also says that no one else mentions his connection with the college of Grassins.

Whatever the exact truth on either point, it is clear that Théru has no substantial evidence here and is masterfully weaving a circumstantial case from presumed associations - bearing in mind that under the Old Regime presumptions could be definitive in cases of sodomy. Voltaire escaped the mercury strands of this man's net, but it is chilling to think how many others – whatever their sexuality – did not:

The abbé Théru to d'Ombreval

[May 1725]

> It is said that sir Arouet de Voltaire is inclined to request the
> release of his dear and intimate friend, the abbé Guyot
> Desfontaines, and that, if he does not dare to do it openly, he will
> use the credit of some people of prestige and authority; but if one

wants to look into the life which this poet has led since he left the Jesuits' college, and if one looks into the people he has frequented, one will pay no attention to his wisdom, nor to those of his friends as very suspect.

In leaving the said college, he was a pensioner at the college of Grassins, and he was there in commerce with several depraved persons, among others with the chevalier Ferrand, old and notorious corrupter, living on the rue de Bièvre, and if one wanted to have him examined, one would find that he has an illness one does not get from writing verse, and the abbé Desfontaines is worthy of being counted among his friends.

121-122

(NOTE: For those who enjoy the resonance of names, the name of Théru's correspondant, Ombreval, then head of the Paris police, suggests "Shadow Valley" in French.)

The first arrest

Ravaisson identifies Desfontaines more precisely as "Pierre-François Guyot Desfontaines, son of a councilor in the Parlement of Normandy, born in Rouen June 22, 1685, died in 1745". The file consists largely of denunciations by the previously mentioned abbé Théru, including some rather defensive protests that, despite his errors of fact, he has the right man. (Ravaisson notes that "N. Théru" was a professor at the college Mazarin.)

Despite Théru's dismissal of Desfontaine's connection with the abbé Bignon – who then ran the *Journal des Savants* – he did in fact have a key function at that publication and his arrest caused some complications in producing the next issue. Bignon's own credit can be measured by the frequency with which his name is raised.

It is amusing today to read Ravaisson's note on the Tuileries:

> The garden of the Tuileries was then covered with hedges and barrel arches which offered convenient refuges for passing encounters; thus at nightfall, debauchees of both sexes installed themselves for the whole evening, and the most outrageous scenes, against good morals, took place there. An outpost of a brigade of the vice police was established there, which made many arrests without being able to end this scandal; the decision was made to tear up the hedges and to demolish the arches.

Apparently, in Ravaisson's time, these measures had been effective. But today the Tuileries has maintained its reputation as a popular gay cruising area.

THE ABBÉ THÉRU, TO D'OMBREVAL

> The abbé Duval des Fontaines, attracts young men to his home to corrupt them, and he often has them sleep with him.

> If one were to look carefully into his conduct, it would be found that he has no or little religion, that he eats meat without need on fast days [!], and that he is involved with small and young libertines, with whom he has parties of debauchery.

He lives on the rue de l'Arbre-Sec, at Notre-Dame-de-Lorette, on the second [*American third*] floor, in front, in a furnished room. He eats, sometimes at the hôtel d'Uzès, rue Jean-Tison, sometimes at the hôtel du Saint-Esprit, rue Saint-Germain; but he can be regarded as a public plague, and it would be good to make an example of him, when these facts have been verified and sir Haymier will do it easily.

Note of M. D'Ombreval - I request that M. Haymier look into it carefully and to give me an account of his findings.

Note of d'Haymier - I have looked into the conduct of the abbé Duval; I have not been able to discover anything about this sodomite; but I have learned that he lives in a rather disorderly fashion, having a woman to his charge, with whom he lives.

INSPECTOR OF POLICE HAYMIER TO THE SAME
September 26, 1724

> *NOTE: Ravaisson lightly redacted this report, with the following footnote:* "D'Haymier braves decency so courageously in words, that we do not dare publish the entire text of his report; we have replaced with dots the most shocking passages." *Anyone who simply MUST read the sordid details can probably find the originals in the Archives Nationales.*

The abbé Duval Desfontaines, living on the rue de l'Arbre-Sec.

As several people have already given memoirs against this abbé, on the subject of infamy, Haymier took care to more particularly investigate his conduct, and in his inquiries, he found a young man, seventeen years old, who knew him perfectly well, and whom he had wanted to debauch since the age of twelve, being at the college of Grassins.....

This young man declared to Haymier that he had met the abbé in the streets a few months ago, that he had recognized him and had given him his address as above, begging him with insistence to go see him in his room, without telling him anything else.

Haymier having judged it appropriate to send the young man this morning to the abbé's, to clarify exactly everything said, with the

necessary instructions to not suffer any indecency on the part of
the abbé, he went there and found him indisposed, without
however being in bed.

After the ordinary greetings, this abbé fell into sordid speech,
asking him how his pleasures were going, telling him that for his
part, he had diverted himself for so long that he was very
weakened and ruined..... that he would give him a half-pistole.

At this moment, the abbé took out of his library engraved books
and figures, full of sodomitical abominations and frightful
positions, which he showed and pointed out one after the other to
the young man, seeming to make much of them.

He further declared to the young man that he did not like to
cavort in the royal gardens, because he knew the consequences;
that, nonetheless, finding himself in the Tuileries the year before,
he had met a young individual..... that same year he had good fun
with a young clerk from Dionis, notary, handsome, blond and
plump, that they often had parties together with other young men
of his acquaintance, and that he often gave the notary's clerk
money; but that he had left him, because he seemed to like
women more than him; that this current year was quite different,
that he did not find himself as vigorous.....

After this long conversation of filth and abomination, the abbé
took the young man to dine with him in his inn, and after they
went their separate ways, [he] telling the young man not to fail to
return with some of his friends.....

Note of d'Ombreval - Arrest him because of his books and his
prints.

THE ABBÉ THÉRU TO D'OMBREVAL
October 8, 1724

One should not bear in Paris, nor leave unpunished sir Duval,
formerly schoolmaster at Chaillot, and who styles himself the
abbé Desfontaines, because it is said he has won a lot in financial
speculation.

If Haymier, police officer, who was charged with observing him, has made a precise report (as is not to be doubted), one should be horrified by his conduct.

The abbé Desfontaines has always been closely linked to M. d'Autruy de Tuisy, living on the rue de Guénégaud, and with M. Haluy, councilor on the great council, who were arrested and taken in the act in the Tuileries by Haymier.

The abbé Desfontaines is a foul individual; he has never been the librarian of M. the abbé Bignon, as he wanted to make M. d'Ombreval and Haymier believe, and he was driven from the Jesuits, because being at Bourges, he refused to do the penitence that his rector imposed on him for diverting himself against the rules; he does not in the least deserve the care taken with him.

October 26, 1724

M. Haymier has told me that the abbé Desfontaines does not bear the name of Duval; but there is no error nor surprise in regarding his person; because he is certainly a foul individual, having attracted and had sleep with him two young men, one named Michault and the other Lamothe. I had only put in my first denunciation the name Desfontaines, his address and the floor he lived on, and where M. Haymier arrested him; I only added the name of Duval in my second memoirs [*sic*], because M. the curé of Saint-Germain, whom I had asked to inquire secretly, had informed me that he was called Duval Desfontaines, that everything I have discovered about this abbé is only too true, and he made me aware that he attracted and received at his home a large number of young men and *petits-maitres* [macaroni *would be one English approximation*]. M. Haymier having sent to the abbé's home a young man he had corrupted, he learned that this foul monster showed him horrible and abominable prints. His host and the neighbors state that he always has around him a crowd of young men, and that the evening he was arrested, he was at the Luxembourg where he found a young man whose suit had silver buttonholes, and that he took him to his place. Thus, it is him that I denounced as a corrupter. M. the parish priest of Saint-Germain, an upright man of great wisdom, will not be able to and cannot deny that, in his note, he had Duval Desfontaines; but it is certain that it is the same person who is criminal, and that there is only an error in the name of Duval and of schoolmaster, speculator, words I was led to add by error, in confirming his hateful foul acts which are in question, which the said abbé will not deny. Thus, the error of an added name does not in the least diminish the truth of the facts which are certain.

If M. d'Ombreval judged it appropriate to commute his sentence and to send him voluntarily to Saint-Lazare instead of Bicêtre, this would be a kindness and a favor of which he will perhaps profit, and for which he will be grateful, although he is not worthy of such an indulgence. M. Haymier will write you his report; but Saint-Lazare suits him better than Bicêtre.

October 28, 1724

I have learned that the abbé Desfontaines calls himself the abbé Bignon's librarian, to get himself out of this business under the shadow of this great name; but the abbé Bignon does not have a librarian, having sold his library to M. Lasse or Law, and before he sold it, he had for librarian a monsieur of your acquaintance. I have warned Haymier of this detail; but it is certain that the abbé Defontaines is a foul individual, that the evening of his arrest he was in the Luxembourg, and that he picked up there a rather decent young man, whom he took to his place, that he was continually with young men and petits-maitres. M. the curé of Saint-Germain-l'Auxerrois, who has gathered and had gathered precise information, regards him as a wretch, and the life he lived in his parish was unworthy and scandalous, thus the name of Duval which has been given him does not diminish in the least his unworthiness, his foul acts, and changes nothing in the person, such that there is no mistake, and no change should be made. It is he whom I have denounced, and who will confess his turpitude, if pressed.

Besides, even if he were the abbé Bignon's librarian, which I deny, even if he were a bishop, he must not be spared; the evil is so great and violent, proportional measures are needed; for example, if the abbé Joisel, councillor in Parlement, had been sent to Saint-Lazare, as well as some people of quality, we would not see anything like as many abominations.

It seems to me people want to save the abbé Desfontaines, and I will tell you more face to face.

[*RAVAISSON'S NOTE: "Despite the abbé Théru's assertions, Desfontaines was set free, after a strong sermon, to which he responded by protestations of repentance and promises to conduct himself better in the future."*]

DESFONTAINES TO HAYMIER
1724

M. the abbé Desfontaines came to have the honor of seeing M. Haymier and to ask him to please come tomorrow morning with M. de Sanec to remove the seals. The *Journal des Savants* must absolutely appear eight days from tomorrow, which is the first Monday of the month. The writings which must be given to the printer are under the seal and have not been able to be finished these last days.

The second arrest

The Bastille's record here centers around the abbé's own interminable letter, half-panicked, half-imperious, to his cousin. While it is more than a little repetitive, it does include useful information, such as the names of people then thought to be the most powerful in this kind of case. Desfontaines himself had a challenging dilemma: to enlist as wide a circle as possible in his cause while hiding the (shameful) fact of where he was.

After the samples of Voltaire's later swipes at Desfontaines which began this subject, it is more than a little surprising to see how much Desfontaines counts (correctly, it seems) on his future enemy's aid. With Voltaire's letter of support (which seems to have been decisive), this and Voltaire's frequent mentions over the years of Desfontaines' ingratitude suggest at the least a more committed friendship than Voltaire later acknowledged. Ravaisson's long note on Voltaire's letter emphasizes this dichotomy:

> One sees that Voltaire did not boast overmuch, when he said that he had gotten his ungrateful critic out of Bicêtre. Who would believe that the same man who wrote so tender a letter on his friend's behalf, could have addressed him the following verses, attributed to him, in the collections of the time:

> 'Adieu, too wicked priest,
> Freed by my credit
> From the castle of Bicêtre,
> For the accursed sin
> Which got his master burned,
> Shameful efforts that I took
> For a ragseller of writing.

> On the hard stool
> Where Duchauffour sat
> When in humble posture
> You appeared the other day
> Fearing the flames
> Where never was seen
> So small a wretch.'

We do not think Voltaire was capable of the filth of which the
abbé Théru accused him, but there are in these verses, as in
everything Voltaire said on the subject of Desfontaines,
something like a cry torn from a great suffering, and that the
pricks to the poet's pride do not sufficiently explain

Note, 122-123

Théru's final note is an entertaining close to the whole affair.
Aside from his sputtering frustration that the abbé has been freed,
it seems to reflect more than a little fear for his own personal
safety. It also includes the useful information that the policeman
Haymier was well-known enough among his quarry to be hated,
and that a person of sufficient rank to act with impunity was not
incapable of avenging his more vulnerable brethren.

Desfontaines himself appears incrementally worse, depending
on the account. For Voltaire, it was enough to mock him as a
sodomite, with all the attendant barbs. The Bastille records
presented by Ravaisson show an unpleasant man, but one who, in
modern terms, was at worst a bit aggressive sexually. It turns out
however that Ravaisson omitted some documents in the case –
perhaps simply because they were not within his scope – which
show Desfontaines arguably committing rape and certainly
engaging in the sort of pimping that takes Chausson and
Deschauffours' behavior, for instance, beyond the bounds of
simple consensual sexual behavior between two parties. The latter
behavior is surprising, since unlike these others, he had another,
more respectable career (as a writer).

Boivin, writing in 1907, uncovered some of these records, the
first of which gives more detail on why Desfontaines found
himself in jail a second time:

April 22, 1725.

Declaration by Louis Legrand, 16 years old, native of Paris and
prisoner at Fort l'Évoque where he was taken by mr. Haymier.

States that eight to ten months ago, while studying drawing and going for the purpose to Mr Luc's Academy, and going out to look for a schoolboy from the Academy of painting at the Louvre, he was accosted by an individual whose name he forgets, who got him to come with him, offering him a collation, that this individual took him to the home of the abbé Desfontaines who then lived in the rue de l'Arbre-Sec ["the street of the Dry Tree"], where he did indeed give him something to drink and during this time suggested to him that they fool around, which they did together, after which he told him that it was too bad that the said abbé Desfontaines was not home, because he could work with him on writing and that he only had to come back that next day, which in fact he did.

That the said day, the sd mr Desfontaines being there and telling him that he had been introduced by the said individual, whom he recognized as his servant, he found himself behind closed doors with the sd master Desfontaines with whom he talked for half an hour, during which the sd mr undid his pants, whipping him in fun and said some things, whose sense he did not then notice, which nonetheless, having seen his writing, he told him to get his father to put him in his home to write, promising him to advance him. That the father of he the speaker having consented to this, the next day he took him to the home of the sd mr abbé Desfontaines, where he stayed for three weeks even drinking, eating and sleeping there, that usually the sd abbé had him sleep with him, from the first day they slept together, the sd sr Desfontaines started toying with him, then threw himself on him... [*probably details are missing here*], that having resisted some, the sd sr Desfontaines lit into him and finally used him with such violence that he entirely achieved his purpose, that he having continued to resist, even because of the pain he suffered, the sd mr abbé having hurt him, they spent part of the night fooling around then fell asleep.

That from that day, despite all the efforts of the sd mr abbé who wanted to get him to again consummate the action, he kept resisting him, having felt too much pain the first time, so that the sd sr abbé Desfontaines satisfied himself with playing with him when they laid together and finally sent him home to his father, forbidding him nonetheless to say that they had slept together. That the sd sr before sending him off, wanting more and more to draw him in, he showed him a little girl who came to his place, urging him to have to do with her, which sd girl is called Babet Taconet and is the daughter of a carpenter who is dead, that her mother lives near the Calvary in the Marais on the side by the boulevard. He knows that the sd girl has to do with the sd mr abbé to whom she gives herself in any way he wants.

Declared that he was taken by the said lackey of mr abbé Desfontaines to the home of the milord André who not finding him to his taste sent him away, after having cavorted with him some time.

Declared further that it is now about a month that he had to do with master Vezou who met him in the rue Traversine and took him to his home nearby; that they consummated the action together, after which he sent him away having given him a twenty-six sols coin.

Declared that about three months ago, being in Versailles, he met Chalal who lives in Paris, on the rue d'Orléans, with whom he also fooled around.

Also has known for a year Favien, lace merchant, who lives in the S' Germain abbey [*meaning the street near it?*], with whom he has often cavorted.

Added the speaker that the sd sr abbé Desfontaines, seeing his resistance, told him that he had had to do with many other young men who had been more compliant that he.

Signed : L. Legrand.

Why Legrand himself was arrested is not said, though (despite his resistance to Desfountaines) he seems to have drifted into prostitution at this point.

At once the lieutenant of police referred this matter to M. de Maurepas with a note the draft of which is in the file.

Duval Desfontaines.

An order was sent on October 18, 1724 to arrest him and take him to the hospital. But as it has been learned since that he is called Guyot Desfontaines, M. the count de Maurepas is asked to have a second order sent from the king under this name; the first is attached.

This is one of the most dangerous sod. there is and who corrupts a number of young people. H.S.H. has so decided. [*S.A.S – Son Altesse Sérénissime – would typically refer to a prince of the blood; it is not clear who is meant here.*]

Henri Boivin, "Les Dossiers de l'Abbe Desfontaines aux Archives de la Bastille (1724-1744), *Revue d'histoire littéraire de la France*, 1907, XCVI:70-71

The Bastille's records continue the story:

MAUREPAS TO D'OMBREVAL

I am sending you the King's orders to have Guyot Desfontaines taken to the hospital.

April 25, 1725

OFFICER HAYMIER TO THE SAME

I have the honor to inform you that, following the King's order, dated last April 25, with which you charged me, I have arrested and taken to the hospital the abbé Guyot Desfontaines. May 2, 1725

THE ABBÉ TO THE SAME
May 2 1725

Over six months ago you had me arrested, and you had me freed the same day. You know that I promised you then, as a man of honor, to never give rise to any new suspicion, and you promised me to pay no more attention to past suspicions. M. the abbé Bignon promised you the same thing on my behalf, and you had told him I would no longer be troubled, if I did not from then on provoke new suspicions. I swear to you that I have been on my best behavior for six months, and that I have not let any young man approach my home. The man I use today for writing, is an old man. Nonetheless, I have been arrested today for an accusation relating to past things, according to the accuser. I have kept my word and I ask you also to keep that which you have given the abbé Bignon. Have the goodness to recall that I am a man with a position, known in Paris, and in all of Europe, by my journal and by other publications. What an awful scandal, if it is known in society the shameful state in which I am; having been very proper for a long time, I did not expect this. Everyone will speak of me as an upright man of good morals. My misfortune is not to be not well-known enough to you, I am persuaded that I would not be dishonored as I am. I beg you to free me as soon as you arrive, no harm has yet been done, if this does not last, but if I stay here long, religion and literature are absolutely dishonored.

P.S. - Note, if you please that I am a man of standing, relative of M. de Novion and allied to M. the abbé Bignon.

THE ABBÉ BIGNON TO THE SAME

Paris, May 4, 1725

In arriving here from Meulan, I learn of the detention of M. the abbé Desfontaines, in regard to which I cannot say more to you than what I had the honor to explain to you on the last occasion; but I am obliged to reclaim for the King's library several books which had been given to him by the *Journal des Savants,* for which he worked. I take the liberty of attaching here the list of these books which I will beg you to have returned to M. the abbé Jourdain, secretary of the library.

Note of M. d'Ombreval - M. Haymier, take a guarantee from the abbé Desfontaines for him to return the books to the library, for which purpose he will authorize someone to be present at the lifting of the seal placed on his effects.

AUTOGRAPH NOTE OF VOLTAIRE

At the home of M. the abbé Desfontaines, rue de Seine, at the hotel of Spain, a volume of Bayle's dictionary and a poem of the league, bound in vellum in -8, with white sheets on each page, filled with handwritten notes.

Note of M. d'Ombreval - This book is requested by M. de Voltaire.

I consent to the two books above being returned to M. de
Voltaire in the presence of M. Sebire Dessaudrayes whom I
commit to be present at the lifting of the seals, this 6th of May,
1725, Desfontaines.

THE ABBÉ DESFONTAINES TO D'OMBREVAL
Bicêtre, May 8, 1725

I have the honor to write you in entering here, and I have
entrusted the officer with my letter.

For 6 months I take God as my witness that I have faithfully kept
the word that I gave you; no suspect young man has been near
me.

The one in question today is among these writers whom I
unfortunately used formerly, and of whom I talked to you with
confidence 6 months ago. For over a year I have not seen him at
all, and he himself agreed in the presence of the police officer;
what is more it is out of the question that I have ever committed
with him the enormous sin nor with anyone at all, of which I am
perhaps accused.

It is not then a question of any new fault; I thought myself safe in
regard to past suspicions, based on your word and my present
conduct.

Have pity on me; do not ruin a man of standing who has some
merit, who has worked so much until now and who has earned
himself some honor in the world; I have infinitely delicate health
and my body cannot long resist the horrors of the prison in which
I am. [RAVAISSON'S NOTE: "The abbé Desfontaines, says
Dargens, was whipped twice a day at Bicêtre. That is true.
Whipping was part of the treatment followed to cure syphilitics
and debauchees."]

You wanted to exile me 6 months ago, exile me now, you will
save my life.

"It is an exile, lord, which my tears ask of you." [*from Racine's*
Andromaque, *Act I, Scene IV*]

I will be obliged to you eternally; if I stay here any longer, I will die or I will go mad; the food, the captivity, the inactivity, the solitude together will attack my body and my spirit. I commend myself to your mercy, and I await all from your compassion; if you deign to do me the honor of speaking to me, that will be a great consolation for me; I must be before your eyes as I was 6 months ago, when you spoke to me with so much goodness; I have not committed the least fault since.

Note of M. d'Ombreval - M. Rossignol, take an order of release and of exile to 30 leagues from Paris. [*This note seems to have been added after the correspondance which follows.*]

THE SAME TO DESSAUDRAYES, LAWYER TO THE
KING'S COUNCILS
May 16, 1725

Here I am, my dear relation and friend, plunged in the greatest misfortune in the world. It is useless to tell you many reasons in order to explain to you the origin; I will only tell you what serves as a pretext for my detention. Keep very secret what I am going to tell you, and save at least honor, though all else be lost for me.

You know that I was arrested, six months ago, and released the same day; it concerned an accusation brought against me on what is called "the cuff" [*a reference to the "Order of the cuff", a slang term for homosexuals*]. It is unthinkable that I would be guilty of this sin, and you know my appearance and my conduct. Nonetheless, I explained then to M. d'Ombreval what gave rise to this accusation, and I promised him to no longer proceed as I had a few times, that is to no longer use young writers who had provoked suspicions and the accusation of my enemies. I have indeed kept the word I had given to M. d'Ombreval, and no suspect young man has approached me *since this time*. I spoke then with much confidence to M. d'Ombreval who spoke to me as well with much kindness. M. the abbé Bignon also promised him the same thing, and matters remained there. I was assured I would no longer be bothered. One of these miserable little persons was caught in recent days, I do not know on what occasion; he was interrogated, and he said that he had once worked for me, but that I had fired him and that I was the cause of his misfortune. This word got me arrested. Nonetheless he has confessed since I have been arrested, in my presence and in the presence of the police officer, that he had not seen me at my home for a year and a half. Effectively I had forgotten so much as his name. You see, my dear friend, that even were I capable of the enormous sin in regard to this foul libertine, which, truly, is not [sic], and what he does not say, that is well before the word I had given to M. d'Ombreval and the affair completed in the month of last October. I am beyond all suspicion, and I even used a man of 40 as a writer when I needed one, as the officer saw when he arrested me; thus 1° I have never committed the sin of sodomy as I am accused of doing; 2° for 6 months I have avoided so much as the shadow of a suspicion, not wanting anymore to use such wretches with an indiscretion for which I am well punished.

That is my situation; once more, defend me in public, if my misfortune is public, but do not go into this sordid detail unnecessarily. I beg you to go find Villette with whom I am reconciled; he lives on the rue Louis-le-Grand, near the place Vendôme, at the home of Le Tellier, captain of the guards; you will find him in the morning; tell him my situation, recommending him to secrecy, and tell him that I beg him to go at once to find M. d'Osmond and Mme Champcenetz to obtain a counter-letter which will free me while answering for my conduct, and let them understand that there is much misunderstanding in this business, and that my enemies have provoked it, because that is true, and there are many things to say about that, which I cannot write. If you go to Versailles with him, you will perhaps speak better. Go find M. de Voltaire, who can make M. de Sully, M. de Richelieu, M. de Maisons, Mme de Prie act upon M. de Maurepas. [*This list of names gives an idea of the influence Voltaire was already thought to have then, and which other writers have said he used on Desfontaine's behalf.*] See also M. Novion in order that he beg Mme de Bernières to solicit Mme de Prie who knows her. See at Versailles M. Hardion, King's secretary, living at the home of M. de Morville to whom I have written, demonstrate my innocence to him in order to make him act willingly with M. de Morville to obtain my freedom or at least my exile, do not be discouraged, when you find hesitations regarding me, because an accused man is almost always guilty in many people's minds. Show that I am a person of standing with some merit, who has spent my life studying and writing, my work, my lifestyle; even were I as guilty as is said, must I serve as an example and be treated like a miserable person? I have been put in Bicêtre like an adventurer, a mountebank, a wretch with no name or reputation.

Go as well, I pray you, to find M. d'Ombreval, do not be surprised by the idea he has of me, he is a worthy man who will listen to reason, note to him that I have been true to my word, because that is the essential point, and that I have not given any reason for suspicion for six months, that he can make as many inquiries as he likes to confirm it; all this is a lot of trouble, but it is a question of saving my life, if I stay here any longer, I will die of pain, of misery and of boredom, because nothing is more horrible than this place, where I have no consolation. Describe to him the delicate state of my health, and try to make him bend.

Get Gèvres and d'Avouet to act in order not to be overwhelmed by so much effort, also the abbé de Fontbriand, I commend myself to all of them, but above all go find the abbé Bignon, who will be in Paris, this week. Show to him that I have kept the word I gave him, that you are sure of it, that all the suspicions have only been formed by my enemies who have poisoned my actions, that the affair in question is old, and that it is being revived, you will find him prejudiced against me, and he imagines that I have caused my own imprisonment by some new indiscretion, which nonetheless is not [true]. Go find him, and engage him to take my defense, if he can, in convincing him of my innocence. See too the abbé Alary my friend, at the home of the president Hénault, place de Vendôme, in order that he speak for me to M. de Fréjus, it is a matter of saving the life of a friend who will perish here, if no one speaks very strongly in his favor, and if no one has pity of his state.

I have taken the liberty of committing you to be present at the lifting of the seals that have been put on my home. Watch that everything is done properly, and be careful that no one touch my books and my papers but the commissioner alone, because it is necessary on this occasion to be very attentive, for fear of surprise and of deception, as you know well, be present in and in official garb, it would be regrettable if a police officer or a clerk got involved, being able to put in what he wants or even rob me, when the seal is removed, you will close my room and my apartment, and take the two keys of the room and the vestibule. Remember that there are two keys for the first door of the vestibule, which are in the hands of the landlord, M. Deshayes, you must take them and lock all my closets. You will take from my library a Hebrew grammar in-8, the 4 volumes of memoirs serving for the history of Europe since 1600, a Juvenal in Latin and French, and a little Latin Horace, and you will take them to your place; you will enter my room after the sealing, when you wish, and you will put there four volumes in-folio which are in the room of my valet where my writer worked, as you will see, a volume of the dictionary of Trévoux is one. You will also take this key.

For the rest, do not divulge publicly at all that I am in Bicêtre, and advise the same to anyone you tell.

When you see M. d'Ombreval, ask for an order as my relation to come see me here. He will not refuse it to you. Bring me, please, some money and the above mentioned books, which you will have taken from my library. It is appropriate that I speak to you, because one cannot say everything in a letter. My only hope is in your efforts and in the zeal of my friends, which you will use. I am not accused of any crime of State, and people can certainly involve themselves in my affairs. If it is not possible to obtain my simple release, it will be necessary to request a letter of exile, but simple release would be better, it is a question of having a counter-letter to lift the letter of cachet. Commit M. de Voltaire, in the name of the friendship he has had for me, to put his powerful friends to work. I even believe he has seen M. d'Ombreval about me, but he must not be discouraged by answers, and neither must you be discouraged. My affair must be pleaded, not only to the powerful, but also to my friends who may be able to help me, because if they consider me as guilty, perhaps they will not hold me in enough esteem to see me again. After all, even if I were (which is certainly not the case), should they abandon me for that? Work, I beg you, with passion and dispatch, and come see the most unhappy of all your friends, plunged into bitterness, into boredom, into misery, who is at present without money and upon the charity of the hospital, locked in a cell like an evildoer, without books, without ink, without occupation, unable, for five days, to eat nor sleep. I await you as soon as possible, but request an order from M. d'Ombreval in writing, which he will not refuse you upon your saying you are my relation, and the only one who can take care of my affairs on the outside. Adieu, my dear relation and friend, do not neglect me.

P. S. I have many things to tell you about my affairs, I will owe you my life, do not delay.

NOTE: *Here is where Théru's letter about Voltaire, already cited in this series, appears in the file.*

VOLTAIRE TO OMBREVAL
Versailles, tuesday morning

I will be obliged to you all my life for what you have been willing to do in favor of the poor abbé Desfontaines, all men of letters who know his superior merit will share my gratitude. If he has been guilty of some indiscretion, he has quite cruelly been punished for it, but I can assure you that he is incapable of the foul crime attributed to him, and that what is more he merits, by his probity, and I dare say by his misfortune, that you give him your protection, and that you deign to speak in his favor to My Lord the duke; you are in a position in which you can do harm, but your heart leads you to do good. For me, I have only thanks to give you, and I join sentiments of the liveliest gratitude to the respect which I have for your person.

Note of M. Duval to M. Rossignol - Give the release order to M. the president de Bernières when he comes to get him.

May 29, 1725

[RAVAISSON'S NOTE: The release order was dated the 24th of May, and Desfontaines left the 30th to go 30 leagues from Paris; at the end of 8 days, he obtained his recall.]

L'ABBÉ THÉRU TO M. D'OMBREVAL'S SECRETARY
June 12, 1725

The abbé Desfontaines is in Paris, and he complains to one and all, proclaiming his innocence, threatening this one and that one; he must confront his accusers, if he can discover who they are; it is a great evil that such a genie remains in this city, where he will find more protectors than the most worthy people.

If one is too careful with corrupters because of their jobs or their families, or their friends, great disorders will result; the officers and those who want to and who must oppose iniquity, will not be safe, and M. d'Ombreval will have troubles and sorrows, because these sorts of persons will take off their masks, thinking everything permitted to them, and will form leagues and clubs which will be noxious, in being led by people of rank. I have already heard of one, and when I am better informed, I will inform our magistrate [*i.e., d'Ombreval*]; but when he acts with indulgence or pardons someone, that person must at least remain calm and correct himself without using violence, threats or vengeance. For example, I would not have wanted to order that the arrest order for sir de Sainte-Colombe be struck out, because this worker can abuse it and make bad use of it in committing [*sic - error for* 'compromising'?] M. D'Ombreval. It would be good to have him secretly observed to know his acquaintances and keep him silent, as well as the abbé Desfontaines. The blows of a stick which a *cordon bleu* [*a Knight of the Order of the Holy-Spirit; that is, an eminent aristocrat*] gave a young man in the Tuileries, at 10-11 in the evening, last Thursday, taking him for M. Haymier, is a convincing proof of what I have just said, and this lord came from the carriage of M. the count de Charolais, and perhaps has already been caught. In a word, one cannot object to the care taken with people of rank, but they must not use violence nor insult the magistrate in the person of his officers; whatever the case, I only regard the public good and good order with the honor of our magistrate.

I am told that the family of abbé Desfontaines would have liked that in leaving Bicêtre he had been ordered to retire into some seminary or well-run community for the rest of his days.

Ravaisson, 1709-1772. XII:102-107; 114-125)

Voltaire looks back

Desfontaines, whose later ingratitude to Voltaire has been widely noted, remained ingratiating when he still needed the philosopher's help:

LETTER FROM the ABBE DESFONTAINES TO M. VOLTAIRE

This 31st of May 1725

I will never forget, Monsieur, my infinite obligations to you. Your good heart is well above your wit, and you are the most essential friend that ever was. The zeal with which you have served me in a way does me more honor that the malice and darkening of my enemies has caused me affront by the unworthy treatment which they have made me suffer. It is necessary to withdraw for some time. *Fallax infamia terret.*

I have a lettre de cachet which exiles me to thirty leagues from Paris. It is with pleasure that I will seek solitude; but I am quite sorry that this retreat has been commanded. It is a remainder of triumph for the miserable authors of my disgrace. I agree to go to the provinces, and I go there quite willingly. But try, Monsieur, to get the king's order lifted by another lettre de cachet in this form:

"The king, informed that the accusation made against the abbe Desfontaines is false, agrees that he stay in Paris."

If you obtain this order from M. de Maurepas, that is an essential move. Further, I promise, *word of honor*, to M. de Maurepas to go at once, and to not return to Paris until I have secretly asked his permission.

There, my dear friend, is what I now ask you to obtain for me. I will still be infinitely obliged to you for this service. It is, I think, what can best be done to repair the scandal and the injustice, while waiting until I can do better, and that I have the necessary insight to uncover the hidden springs of the horrible intrigue of my enemies. Despite the darkness of the accusation and the tendency of the public to think all accused persons guilty, I have the satisfaction of seeing even indifferent people take my part. The Nadals, the Danchets, the Depens, the Frérets, are the only ones, it is said, who treat my person as all my life I will treat their filthy works and their unworthy character. *Genus irritabilevatum.*

I have a plan for a defense which will be fine and curious, and which I will work on in the country. I am too known in the world for a man like me to be silent after so execrable an affront; and I will do it so that I will have the honor of presenting it to M. de Maurepas, to ask him to allow me to publish it. Every misfortune which has occurred to me will then be seen, along with my miseries always caused by literary people, above all the story of my leaving the Jesuits.

Adieu, my dear friend; I commend myself to you.

DESFONTAINES

These may have been the last kind words between them. Desfontaine's later attacks on his one-time protector are more referenced than quoted and it would be tedious to reproduce all of Voltaire's subsequent jibes at Desfontaine.

Probably his most famous remarks on this case and that of Deschauffour's (which follows) are in the Philosophical Dictionary, under the article "Socratic Love", where they appear in a long footnote. The article itself, and the note that follows this one, are both effectively tirades against homosexuality (the second notes begins: "Permit us to make several observations on a hateful and disgusting subject, but one which unfortunately is part of the history of opinions and manners").

Even Voltaire seems to allow for "extenuating circumstances":

Young males of our species, raised together, feeling this force which Nature is beginning to unleash in them, and not finding the natural object of their instinct, turn to what is like it. Often a young man, by the freshness of his complexion, by the brilliance of his coloring, and by the sweetness of his eyes, looks for two or three years like a beautiful girl; if one loves him, it is because

nature is confused; or pays homage to the sex, in attaching itself
to what has its beauties; and when age has made this
resemblance fade, the confusion ends.

The ex-Jesuit Desfontaines was about to be burned in the Grève
having abused a few small chimneysweeps who reamed his
chimney; protectors saved him. A victim was needed;
Deschaufours was burned in his place. That is quite something;
est modus in rebus; one must fit the punishment to the crime.

A bit strangely, Voltaire then goes on to explain that the
penalties against "buggers" were originally intended for heretics
and that the ambivalence of the term "bugger" (*bougre,* derived
from a word for Bulgarian, then referring to heresy) led to a fatal
misunderstanding:

What would Ceasar, Alcibiades, Nicodemus the king of
Bithnyia, Henri III the king of France and so many others have
said? In burning Deschaufours, it was based on the
Etablissements de saint Louis, put in new French in the XVth
century. "If anyone is suspected of b..., he must be taken to the
bishop; and if it is proved, he must be burned, and all his
furniture are the baron's, etc." Saint Louis does not say what
must done to the baron, if the baron is suspected, and it is
proved. It must be noted the by the word of b..., Saint Louis
meant heretics, who were called by no other name. An
ambivalence led to Deschaufours, a gentleman of Lorraine, being
burned in Paris. Despréaux was quite right to write a satire
against ambivalence; it has caused more harm than is thought.

Presumably, Voltaire's last remark about "Deschaufours" is
merely an exercise in wit. As will now be seen, little in the
Deschauffours case was ambivalent.

The Deschauffours case

NOTE: the name is spelled differently in different accounts.

The Deschauffours case was one of the more spectacular sodomy cases of the Old Regime, but is under-represented in the more general contemporary sources (which probably reflects the period's reticence on this subject in general and on this wide-ranging case in particular.) The *Gay, Lesbian, Bisexual, Transgender & Queer Encyclopedia* says: "The most famous homosexual condemned to death in this era was undoubtedly Étienne-Benjamin Deschauffours (d. 1726), a pimp for men who sought sex with other men, who was burned at the stake for child abuse and murder." Another modern summation differs slightly, but gives more detail:

> Under a variety of pseudonyms, and in various lodgings, Deschauffours earned a living by spotting 'likely lads' and supplying them on payment of commission to wealthy clients, both French and foreign (perhaps some 200 in all). Deschauffours frequently tried out his finds (young and very young), and found his pleasure in their pain (it is difficult not to think forward to the Marquis de Sade, or backward to Gilles de Rais). He castrated a young Italian whose admirer hoped this might render him more compliant.

> Robert Aldrich, Garry Wotherspoon, *Who's who in gay and lesbian history: from antiquity to World War II, Routledge*, 2003; 148.

Here is a modern comment on Voltaire's view of the case:

> When Voltaire wrote regarding the execution of the foul Etienne Benjamin Deschauffours, burned alive May 24, 1726 on the place de Grève, when he agrees with "suiting the punishment to the crime", he commits a singular gaffe - misinformed? or else he badly dodges the issue while playing the game of power, and playing the fine role, this time, for a bad cause.

Because it is not a question of another Calas, or Sirven, or La
Barre case. Deschauffours, a character who prefigures the heros
of Sade, was convicted of kidnapping, pandering, child rapes,
attack on corporal integrity (castration), and murder... But the
commission constituted by the King's order, judging in last resort
(the process thus not allowing an appeal to Parlement) only
retained the crime of sodomy. Condemnation equals example
and, renewing a usage long fallen into disfavor, the Lieutenant
General of Police had it announced and posted in the streets of
Paris.

Gérald Hervé in Hervé Baudry's *LA NUIT DES OLYMPICA-Essai sur
le national-cartésianisme*, PAGES CHOISIES (IV) Collection
Ouverture Philosophique, L'Harmattan, 1999

The last comment is questionable - this "usage" was continued in
several other cases at least. But it is certainly true that
Deschauffours' case was presented to the public as one of
sodomy, and has gone down into history as such, when in fact it is
far more one of rape, child abuse and pandering. It is not an
exaggeration to call Deschauffours a monster, a man who
snatched a child out of his parents arms and beat one (perhaps the
same) to death, who casually castrated a young man with the
futile hope of giving him a good voice, who probably kidnapped
another whom he had already raped... Etc. The details which
follow are often quite disturbing, and one can only wish that,
whatever his sexual preference, Deschauffours had been caught
and stopped far earlier.

The case expanded to include a number of figures, only some
of whom were arrested.

Barbier's famous Journal gives an overview of the case that is
accurate as far as it goes, though it only hints at the real crimes
that led Deschauffours to the stake:

For quite some time this vice has reigned in this country, and
recently it is more in fashion than ever. All the young lords
furiously engage in it, to the great sorrow of the women of the
Court. Four or five months ago a certain Des Chaufours was put
in the Bastille, an individual in Paris, great b..... by trade, a
handsome man and well made. This man knew many people in

the great world and the mediocre, because, in general, this is not an amusement for the petit bourgeois. His place was where people met, debauchery went on there. Finally, this was discovered, I do not know how, what is more, a list has been had of all the participants in this debauchery, which includes over two hundred people of every rank. This has made for quite an affair. The King has named M. the lieutenant of police and some councilors from the Châtelet as commissioners to judge in last resort, the King's procurer, Moreau, as general prosecutor of the commission. Horrible things have been seen in this trial where complete proof has been found. Several people have been taken who have been locked up, sent to the islands. It has even been said that this would be quashed, but the thing has seemed too serious. M. Hérault wanted and made it understood that it was necessary to make an example, that it was not possible to punish all those discovered, because that would cause too much trouble. And besides it would not take much more to illustrate this crime and make it more common, most people here not knowing what it is. DesChaufours [*sic*] was the most guilty, because it was he who held these secret parties. And his trial done, he was taken last night from the Bastille to the Châtelet. Yesterday morning, he was questioned on the stool [*a literal but also symbolic stool – la sellette – used for questioning criminals; sometimes loosely but evocatively translated as "the hot seat"*] for the crime of sodomy, judged and condemned to be burned alive. He was executed in the afternoon, on the Grève square, with the difference that he was first strangled. There has not been an execution for this crime in a long time, and that will keep a little in line those tainted with this crime against nature; because otherwise there is no civil reparation to be made at all. He had a brother-in-law, provincial commissioner of war, who even had received king Stanislas on his passage and had regaled him, who asked for his pardon; but as this crime is becoming common and this man held an academy for it, they wanted to make an example....

It is said that with Des Chaufours in the Bastille was a certain Nattier, painter, who cut his own throat. The abbé de La Fare, bishop of Laon, was in this company; he is locked up in a seminary. M. the count de Tavannes, a *cordon bleu*, is, it is said, exiled for the same reason. Regarding the abbé de Saint-Aignan, bishop of Beauvais, he has for a prison the novitiate of the Jesuits, and so it is clear that it is not for the same cause, it is for debauching women.

Barbier, May 1726, (Charpentier, 1857-1866) I:425-426

Note that numerous other names appear in different accounts. One reason a special commission was assigned for the case was precisely because, as in the Affair of the Poisons (for which such commissions were created), the authorities wanted to avoid publicizing certain names involved (and in fact, over a hundred years later, Ravaisson still showed a similar concern in reprinting the archives involved.)

The inequality of treatment was again not lost on satirists and the public. A satire from 1734 (in the *Recueil de Maurepas*) was sung to a tune called "There's the difference" ("Voilà la différence"):

Du Chauffour and d'Oswal
are two unparalleled buggers,

There's the resemblance.

One burned for his crime,
the other was made cardinal,

There's the difference.

A period writer, Bois Jourdain says:

M. Delpech, counselor to the parlement of Bordeaux, was given to the same vice. He was exiled to Toulouse by an order of the king of July 4, 1723; but instead of obeying, he still stayed at Deschaufours'; he was part of all his gatherings; he was ultimately forced to go to the place of his exile. He is currently master of requests.

Bois Jourdain is not entirely dependable however (though he may reflect accurately reflect certain rumors of the time). The trial record shows that the case broke when a mother filed a complaint about her son's rape; nowhere does it mention any family for Deschauffours (who is said several times to hate women). But Bois Jourdain's account, sometimes quoted elsewhere, says:

He was son of a man who had formerly been the director of franchises at Mans, and who by his prodigious spending died, like his wife, in misery. He left four children: this one, who had been a lieutenant in the regiment of Tesse; another son, who was a canon in Mans, and who is dead, driven from the chapter for his debauchery; a daughter, married to M. Aubron, war commissary, and finally *commissaire-ordonnateur* [financial commissary], who left two daughters, of whom one married sir Riouffe, son of a very rich man of Cannes, and who gained the office of *commissaire-ordonnateur*.

Deschauffours' other sister is known in the world of debauchery by the name of the marquise de Barville.

He was married, and while he was being burned, his wife was at the home of a gentleman of Normandie, a very depraved man. He left a son and two daughters, who were at his home when he was arrested, and who were sent to the home of their maternal grand-father.

He was madame de Mortaigne's joint guardian.

It is said that a lackey, named Arbaleste, turned him in. He had beat him; this valet roughly took his revenge; Deschauffours had him arrested. Arbaleste, to escape the punishment, revealed his master's doings.

No person by this name appears in the transcript, but this bit of satire shows that others too accepted this version:

EPITAPH

You gave, Arbaleste, a faithful report:
The [female] sex triumphs at last, and Deschaufours is dead.
The order of the cuff loses in him its true father,
He played host to the butt-boys of Paris.
But in the Luxembourg all his dispersed camp
Left him in the hands of a treacherous policeman.
He had the virtue of Pompeius' son-in-law;
Everyone mourns him, both church and sword.
And this leader who himself alone has, for forty years,
Borne what France had of important ---,
And who, in his hideaway, despising fortune,
Took vengeance on his equals for the common quarrel,
Dies and leave behind him, to avenge his death,
Large --- and small --- which do not match.

De Bois Jourdain, *Mélanges historiques, satiriques et anecdotiques de M. de B. Jourdain*, Chevre et Chanson, 1807; 336-338.

("The Order of the Cuff" apparently was an actual club at one point but became a winking term for homosexuals; the redacted words can probably be guessed; "the common quarrel" seems to mean the battle of the sexes.)

As it happened, just as Deschauffours was being burned, the Jesuit college on the rue St. Jacques caught fire. M. Godeau, a parish priest, was probably not the only one to think that the school had something in common with the condemned man, but he was the one put in the Bastille two days later on suspicion of having written the following quatrain:

When Deschauffours was burned
For the philosophical sin,
The fire, by sympathy,
Spread as far as Loyola.

He was then exiled to Corbeil. "The joke is that this parish priest favored the same vice and that he had for a long time sought a position from the Principal of the college, in order to practice it more easily." (Bois Jourdain)

Ravaisson's list of those put in the Bastille gives some idea of how extensive the case was:

GASPARD [*Entry order of December 17, 1725 and of exit of June 28, 1726*]; NATTIER [*Entry order of December 31, 1725, died April 27, 1726*]; LEFEBRE [*Entry order of December 31, 1725 and of exit of July 28, 1726*]; DUCHAUFOUR [*Entry order of December 31, 1726 and of exit of July 22, 1726*] ; DE MORNARD [*Entry order of January 17, 1726 and of exit of July 22, 1726*] ; LEGRAND , POTAIL, DUBOIS, MASSON , FLORISEL, LEGRAS [*Entry order of January 17, 1726 and of exit of May 20, 1726*]; DE LA R.... [*Entry order of January 17, 1726 and of exit of August 6, 1731*]; HÉBERT [*Entry order of February 7, 1726*]; LOUIS [*Entry order of February 23, 1726 and of exit of September 3, 1726*]; RENAUDOT [*Entry order of April 9, 1726 and of exit of February 26, 1726*]; LABOUREUR [*Entry order of May 17, 1726*]; HAMON [*Entry order of May 19, 1726*]; M----- [*Entry order of November 8, 1726*]

("Exit" did not necessarily mean release – it could refer to a transfer or even an execution.) Curiously, Duchaffours (Duchaufour)'s entry date is well after his initial arrest (on July 18, 1725). Yet he was taken immediately to the Bastille at that point. This may an error in transcription, or perhaps indicates some unknown change after his arrest. For now it can only be noted.

Ravaisson, in transcribing these files, says frankly that he has removed certain family names to protect their descendants. He also redacts the more graphic details, leading to some frustrating lacunae. His standard approach is to offer the Bastille records (and any related ones he found) chronologically. (Ravaisson, 1726-1737 XIV:49-61). The record includes several cases beyond Deschauffours' and some of what follows has been reorganized to group related cases.

The Bastille file begins with a quote from the Savonarola-like Abbé Thèru. This piece is undated and appears to refer to Riotte de la Riotterie, whose case appears later here and in fact is not discussed otherwise until later in the file:

THE ABBÉ THÈRU TO HÉRAULT.

It is suggested that M. Hérault carefully reread the declaration that Verdun gave in order that this wise judge may without committing himself order what the glory of God, justice and the public good demand, by intimidating some, by warning others or their family; some of them, like the commissioner R. of L. M. deputized for the commerce of La Rochelle; M. counselor; H. clerk; the abbé d'A. and the abbé de P.

If one wants to examine the life of La R., it will be found detestable and one will be convinced that he is a pernicious citizen. It will not be enough to have cited and interrogated him, because nothing will be gained; but being famous among the filthy, it will be appropriate to send him to jail.

Sir de la Lanière will readily know his residence and quickly verify these facts. (B. A.)

The record continues with one other later note before providing a few pieces on Deschauffours himself, followed by items concerning others arrested in the case.

Deschauffours

Deschaffours was not the only defendant in the case that bears his name, but the surviving record reflects his central role in it. The trial transcript (in French, simply "the trial" (*le procès*)) was theoretically burned along with him, but, intentionally or not, a copy was preserved and is almost entirely reproduced by Hernandez. It is very long, in fact almost a booklet in itself, and it has been tempting to redact it here. However, not only does the sweep of the various depositions provide an unusual glimpse into a largely hidden aspect of Old Regime life, these are filled with the kind of vivid details which draw many readers to such first-hand accounts; clothes, trades, colorful names, they are all here.

Deschauffours himself, repellent as he is, is drawn as clearly as any character out of Dickens. Others, if they are not as frankly evil, appear as less than savory. There is his opportunistic, amoral valet, Picard, or a surgeon who loses all interest in a boy's fate when told he is a bastard. A widow's tears are touching until she reveals how she soon wanted to remarry, and whom – she'd set her sights on Picard, even as he regaled her with tales of the men he'd slept with. Admirable figures appear as well, notably the Irish surgeon who cares for his neighbor's son for free, and in fact brings the case to light, or a priest who, though horrified by his parishioner's actions, shows concern for his welfare as well. There is also the poignant case of a servant who hears a boy being badly beaten, but – probably because she is a servant – does not dare intervene, yet goes after to follow the boy's condition at the hospital. Her caution appears justified when one then sees that another servant, trying to warn a father, is almost beaten for her pains.

Such considerations may explain why so much of this went unreported. Ironically, the testimony shows too how much de facto tolerance existed for behavior that was so often cited with ostentatious horror. Witness after witness says, almost casually, that not only was it commonly known that Deschauffours was a sodomite, but even that he was a panderer – at the least. Yet it took not only extreme behavior but the accident of one victim living in the same building with a sworn surgeon for a man had who kidnapped more than one child and raped several young men to be so much as arrested.

As a practical matter, far from being quick to condemn, many in this case seemed to be tolerant to a fault.

The initial charge

The story outlined in this initial complaint (which is rarely reproduced, even in part, in French or English) is horrifying enough. Yet it was merely the start of an increasingly horrible saga.

CRIMINAL TRIAL TRANSCRIPT OF BENJAMIN DESCHAUFFOURS, ACCUSED AND CONVICTED OF SODOMY AND OF HAVING MADE OTHERS COMMIT THE SAID CRIME OF SODOMY AND OTHER GREAT AND ATROCIOUS CRIMES, AND BURNED FOR THIS REASON IN THE PLACE OF THE GREVE, May 25, 1726.

In the year seventeen hundred twenty five, this day Monday the second day of the month of July, in the presence of ourselves, Jean Etienne de L'Espinaye, King's counselor, Inquiring Commissioner attached to the police of the saint Germain des Prez district, appeared Marie Geneviève Anquetil, widow of Robert Finet, clockmaker when living, complainant for Henry Hillaire Finet, her son and that the said Robert Finet, the said Henry Hillaire Finet also present. Which Hanquetil told us that Sunday the first of the present month, the said Henry Hillaire Finet having gone to the house of the said Deschauffours to take a watch which the said Deschauffours gave him the previous Monday to fix a spring in it, he went around ten thirty in the morning into a house on the rue de Bussy [*Buci*] and went up to the first apartment occupied by the said sir Deschauffours, who had him go into the said apartment, and after told him he was very happy with his work, told him to go into his study, where he wanted to give him lunch, the complainant adding that the said Henry Hillaire Finet, her son, not daring to enter, the said sir

Deschauffours gave him a small slap on the cheek laughing, and
said, in taking him by the arm: "Go in then, little rascal, you're
making me insist," and then the said Finet having entered the
said study with a view of the courtyard, he found a table laid out,
with a cold fowl, another dish, with several bottles of wine on it,
and around the table were seated two individuals of which one
was dressed in brown silk and the other in black ras de Saint Mor
[*Maure*]; that the said individual dressed in brown silk then told
him: "Come in, my child, and come sit next to me." That the said
Finet, not daring to disobey sat a bit away from the said
individual dressed in brown silk, which individual had him come
nearer, and gave him a glass, which he filled with wine, and at
the same time gave him a bit of the roast fowl which was on the
table; that the said Finet, urged on by the said individuals and by
the said sir Deschauffours, drank the said glass of wine, and after
a brief quarter of an hour felt sleepy, and finally without being
able to help it fell asleep in the presence of the said individuals;
that the said Finet waking around twelve thirty, nearly one,
found no one in the said study, and found himself laid out on the
floor, his suit and pants torn and covered with blood; that getting
up and arranging himself as best he could, he knocked at the
door of the said study and called out; at which noise the said sir
Deschauffours came running and seemed shocked seeing him so
racked and in such disarray, and asked him how he got in that
state; that the said Finet answered that the said sir Deschauffour
must know more about it than anyone else, since it seems that the
two individuals who were in the said study had put him in this
state; at which the said sir Deschauffours answered that he was
wrong to accuse honest people who came to his house and who
had far more reason to complain of his idiocies and
impertinence, since, the said Deschauffours added, the said Finet
had drunk so much that he got drunk and had committed a
hundred impertinences, and had undone his pants in front of
everyone, and his suit, and that he, seeing this, had made many
excuses to the said individuals, who went out at that moment,
saying that one should never put the little people, capable of such
crudity, at one's table; the said complainant adds that the said
Finet at once left the said house and came back to her place,
telling her everything that happened, and the words of the said sir
Deschauffours; upon which she asked sir Taylor, surgeon living
in the house where she lodges, to come up and see the condition
of her son, who seemed to really be hurt, that he immediately
wrote up a statement, to provide a report to whom it may
concern, etc.

Today Tuesday the third day of the month of July, appeared in our presence, David Edward Taylor, Surgeon sworn expert received at Saint Cosme, who declared to us that in obedience to our summons brought to him yesterday evening, he came to know what we wanted of him; upon which we read him the current complaint presented yesterday by the woman named Anquetil; after which we asked the said sir Taylor if it was true that last Sunday he had applied the first dressing on the said Finet, which Taylor, after having sworn to tell us the pure and sincere truth, told us that, last Sunday, around two in the afternoon, he was called to examine and see if the one called Finet was wounded; upon which he went into a room on the third floor at the rear, in the house of which he is the principal tenant, on the rue des Mauvais Garçons ["*street of the Bad Boys*"], in the suburb of Saint Germain and found the said Finet stretched out on a bed, the said Finet complained of a great pain in his behind, and at the same time told him everything that had happened, after which the said Taylor carefully examined the said Finet, and found and recognized that the said Finet had a torn anus, and that there was every appearance that he had been raped and known carnally against nature, upon which he, respondent, had put the appropriate dressings on the wound, which besides did not seem very dangerous.

The first witnesses

Today Monday, the sixteenth day of July, two hours after noon, in the presence of ourselves, Camuzet, King's councilor, Inquiring Commissioner, attached to the police of the saint Jean en Grève district, appeared in person the individuals indicated below, whom we have questioned in the following manner:

First witness.

The first of them was an individual dressed in a suit of mixed gray drugget, carrying a lace wig, with a cane, who responded that he was named Jean Petit, called Painque, that he was Burgundian, native of Bar sur Seine and came to Paris at eighteen, where he went into service with sir Tourton, Banker, living there on the rue saint Martin, and then entered that of sir Deschauffours, living then on the rue des Bons Enfants [*"street of the Good Children"*], near the Palais-Royal gate, which Deschauffours then had himself called master Moulien Duplessis, and that having left this master in 1721, he went into the service of master Le Boisauvert, trader in La Rochelle, who was then staying in Paris, and at whose death he remained without a position; answered that he was thirty one.

Asked if in the time that he stayed at the house of the said Deschauffours he noticed anything and bad doings, answered that he saw no woman or girl come there, but lots of decent young men and well presented.

Asked if there were not poorly dressed people who came as well, answered that he often saw young handsome and well-made boys whom master Deschauffours treated very well, also others who then came, in the evening, and that sometimes the said persons of good standing slept and passed the night at the home of the said sir Deschauffours.

Asked if he did not know if something happened against decency, towards the said young boys, answered that he had heard it said that the said sir Deschauffours was thought to maintain a shameful trade in sodomy, that he never saw any sign of it but what he said above, except that he heard a very well-dressed lord who told master Deschauffours that the boy he proposed to him was not well-shaped enough, that he had examined him and wanted none of him; upon which he the respondent said the next day to the said master Deschauffours that apparently the said lord did not want to take the boy just as his valet, since although he was was big and good-looking, he did not find him shapely enough, and he found it rather extraordinary that one had a lackey undress to see naked if he was well made; upon which the said master Deschauffours answered that this lord was capricious and mad; but that, after eight days, the said master Deschauffours, apparently displeased that his secret was known, released him from service, on the pretext that he wanted to spend two or three months in the country, where he had no need of lackeys.

Asked if he knew the names of those who frequented the house of the said Deschauffours, answered no, and that besides so many people came there that he could not have remembered the names, that he only knew that the lord of whom he had just spoken and who refused the young man, whom the said master Deschauffours offered him, was Monsieur the Marquis de Sautereau.

Asked if he knew the name of the said young boy, answered that he had never heard him named, that only knew he was the son of a tapestry maker who lived on the rue Tire-boudin ["*Pull-sausage street*"].

Asked if the said sir Marquis de Sautereau often came to the house of the said master Deschauffours, answered that he had seen him there three or four times.

Second Witness.

In continuing which we had approach an individual dressed in rust-colored cloth, carrying a hat embroidered with silver, and a sword, which individual answered that he was named Regnault Poitret, called Musicien ["Musician"], that he was from Nancy in Lorraine, that he was forty-six and that he had been enlisted in the Regiment of the Gardes françoises, Colonelle Company.

Asked if he knew Deschauffours, answered yes.

Asked if he knew or had knowledge that the said Deschauffours had or maintained some bad activity, answered that he had known the said master Deschauffours in the time when he lived on the rue Poupée [*"Doll Street"*], near the rue de Hautefeuille, and had himself called the Marquis du Preau, that the so-called Marquis du Preau was lodged in a furnished apartment and had in his service two young and well-shaped lackeys, and to whom he was very attentive, that one of the said lackeys, called Picard, being one day in a quarrel with the said so-called Marquis de Preau told him in the presence of him, respondent, that he absolutely wanted to quit, and that also he put up with things for him that went against his conscience and that if they were known they ran no less risk one than the other of being burned, on which the said so-called Marquis de Preau gave him twelve crowns that he owed him and told him that he would never find so good a household as his; adding the said respondent that the said Picard having gone out, the said Marquis de Preau told him that this lackey was a very good lad but that he was given to fantasy, and at the same time, that he had moments of mental trouble, where he said things with no sense to them.

[*Note that, a bit weirdly, these two lackeys' names were Picard and La Fleur, while Chausson had had a valet named Picard who was nicknamed... "La Fleur". To confuse matters further, a woman who appears later in the case was nicknamed "La Picarde" (both were very probably from Picardy).*]

Asked at which time the said Deschauffours lived on the rue Poupée and had himself called the Marquis de Preau, answered that it was in 1719, that the said so-called Marquis de Preau, having won some wealth in the system [*of John Law; that is, a speculation*] had taken the said furnished apartment and the said two lackeys.

Asked if he knew what became of the said Picard, answered that he had never had any news of him, nor met him, and that he had heard it said that the said Picard went into service with a Prussian lord, in which country he went with him, and finally enlisted with the troops of the King of Prussia, which things the respondent nonetheless said he did not dare to confirm, having only heard them second hand, but that he nonetheless thought them true.

Asked if he knew the name of the other lackeys in service with the said Deschauffours, answered that the said second Lackey was named La Fleur, that he knew that La Fleur had left the said Marquis de Preaux soon after the said adventure, and went to Montargis, place of his birth, where he was presently established as a cooper, and was rather well married with the widow of a cooper.

Asked if he knew if the said La Fleur had had criminal relations and carnal and sodomitical habitation with the said Deschauffours, answered that he knew nothing about that and had heard nothing, that what is more La Fleur had always seemed to him a very well-behaved boy, and very peaceful, and even devout.

Asked if he knew something more than what he had said, the which Regnault Poitret answered us that he knew no more than what he had just said, given that he had only frequented the said Deschauffours for his business, having then dealt in silk stockings and thread.

Third Witness.

In continuing the said interrogation we had approach an individual dressed in cinnamon-colored cloth and carrying a cane, which individual said that he was called Arnaud Daniel Perron, that he was Burgundian, born near Charolles, that he was thirty-five, and that he was a waiter at the tavern of sir Thomas Buffet, Wineseller, living on the rue du Four, Saint Germain suburb.

Asked if he knew Deschauffours, answered yes.

Asked he knew or had knowledge of the said Deschauffours' having any bad dealings, answered that he knew that the said Deschauffours was a sodomite and committed the said crime against nature, since one day he, respondent, going to his place to bring there twenty four bottles of wine that he had paid for, the said Deschauffours, after having been very nice to him, and asked if he did not have a mistress, he answered that he did not want one, given that a mistress demanded too much care, and often acted difficult and nagged, and with that made you spend a lot of money; upon which the said Deschauffours told him that he wanted to get him a lover who instead of costing him money would provide him with it infinitely, and that with this lover he would not run the risk of getting sick as with a whore; upon which the respondent, having responded that if he did not risk his purse or his health, he ran a much greater risk, which was that of being burned and of dying a shameful death, and that besides he had never, thank God, had the inclination and leaning for this act against nature; upon which the said Deschauffours answered, and wanted to prove to him with very fine reasons that there was nothing criminal in this intercourse; but that he, respondent, not wanting to listen to him, left his house rather brusquely, and promised him nonetheless to not speak of what just happened.

Asked if the said Deschauffours had done or wanted to do him any violence, answered that the said Deschauffours being then alone, and he, respondent, being much stronger and more robust than he, he would not have feared his violences, and also that he did not go to that excess, being happy to try to seduce him with his fine words.

Asked if he knew to whom the said Deschauffours wanted to provide him, answered that the said Deschauffours named no one, and only told him that he wanted to introduce him to a great lord of the finest sort, without nonetheless telling him his name.

Asked if he knew that the said Deschauffours, not content with running a trade in sodomy and having this crime committed, did not commit it himself as well, answered that he did not know exactly, but that the said master Deschauffours was thought to be such, and even that it was said that he knew carnally all these persons that he so provided, to try them out, which he nonetheless did not dare to affirm, having very little frequented the said master Deschauffours, and had not wanted to return to his place since the above incident.

4th Witness.

In continuing which interrogation we had approach an individual wearing a dress of blue and white siamoise, which individual said she was called Jeanne Elisabeth, called Big Jeanne, that she was the daughter of Mathurin Cordelier, winegrower, and of

Charlotte Bonvalet, his wife, that she was from Gien, near Sully, that she did not know her age exactly but she had been told that she was only four when her father died, and that her said father died on Saint Pierre's day in 1683, the same year the Queen died, and so she must presently be forty five to forty six years old; that she was a servant at the house of Marie Angard, widow of Pierre Doreau, who let out furnished rooms, living in Paris, on the rue Poupée, near the rue Hautefeuille.

Asked if she knew Deschauffours, answered no.

Asked if she had known Deschauffours five or six years ago when he was called the Marquis du Preau answered yes.

Asked if she knew or had knowledge of the said so-called Marquis du Preau carrying on some bad dealings, answered that the said Marquis du Preau stayed over eighteen months with the above-named Angard, widow Doreau, in the above-mentioned furnished hotel on the rue Poupée, that he had two big lackeys in his service, that he saw very respectable people, and always new faces; that the above-mentioned lackeys of whom one was called Picard and the other La Fleur were very familiar with him, and above all the said Picard, who did not stop threatening the said Marquis du Preau that he would leave him, that what is more the said Marquis du Preau was a very nasty man, who mortally hated girls and women, and ran after young boys, often having into his place chimney-sweeps and bootscrapers, whom he gave good suppers and whom he had sleep in his bed; that it was said in the neighborhood that he slept with them as with a mistress; also came to the home of the said Marquis very well dressed people, to spend entire after-dinners, with young men, but there were never girls among them.

Asked if she did not notice anything more specific, answered yes, and that one day on a date she has forgotten, there was a lot of company, and among others three or four lords with young men of good family; that on this day, the said Picard, lackey, having told La Fleur his friend to come drink with him in a tavern at the corner of the said rue Poupée and of the rue de la Harpe, and the said La Fleur having said that he could not leave, given that perhaps Monsieur the Marquis might call him and have need of him, the said Picard had answered: "Come, come, our Master and the people with him have quite other concerns.

They cannot leave each other, and are all stuck to each other like maybugs." Upon which they went out; adding the said respondent that another time, in the morning, the said Marquis had brought a very handsome young man, blond, to his home, after which the said Picard went with him into the study at the rear, and she had heard arguing, and the said boy crying out he was being killed; that this noise and these cries having lasted some time, the said boy finally came out of the said Marquis' apartment, face quite red, and adjusting his outfit, and said in the staircase: "Here is a great wretch! I would never have suspected this treason, and this rascal of a lackey will pay for it!", that nonetheless, after five or six days, the said young boy returned to the home of the said Marquis, and frequented him rather often for a month, at the end of which time the said young boy no longer appeared at the house.

Asked if she knew the name of the said young boy, answered yes, that the said boy was the son of a tailor living on the rue du Foin ["*Hay Street*"], called Duplan.

Asked if she knew what happened to Duplan *fils*, answered yes, and it was said that the said son of Duplan had gone with an English lord who had seen him at the home of the said Marquis Du Preau where he went very often.

Asked if she knew the name of the said English lord, answered no, but she had known rather closely one of the lackeys who had served the said English Milord, who told her that this Englishman was a very rich and good Milord, but that girls had nothing to fear from him, nor anything to gain, given that he only liked boys, and that he only came to the home of the said Marquis Du Preau to beg him to introduce him to some handsome blond, for whom he wanted to do some good, and that he hoped the boy would be of a mind to come with him into his country of Scotland.

Asked if she knew the name of the said lackey, answered yes and that he was called Dubois.

Asked if she knew where the said Dubois was at present, answered no, but that she nonetheless thought he was in service in Paris.

Asked if she also knew the names of some people who had
frequented the house of the said Marquis Du Preau, answered
that she knew that Monsieur the Count of ---- came there
sometimes, as well as Monsieur de la Tour de Tessam, and a
King's secretary who came more often, and Monsieur the
Marquis de Sautereau *fils*, that she had also seen there a single
and unique time.

Asked if she had heard after of the said so-called Marquis du
Preau, answered yes, and that she had also been told that he had
been arrested for the crime of sodomy, but she did not know that
it was the same person as master Deschauffours.

5th witness

In continuing the said interrogation we had approach an
individual dressed in brown tiretaine who said he was named
Thomas Vaupinesque, called Chambery, that he was from
Annecy in Savoy, that he was a dock hand and that he was
sixteen and a half.

Asked if he knew Deschauffours, answered yes, and that two
years ago the said master Deschauffours meeting him in the rue
de l'Arbre sec [*"street of the dry Tree"*] told him that he wanted
to have him deliver some messages and that he seemed skillful
enough; that he, respondent, having followed the said master
Deschauffours to his house, which was in the rue Platrière on a
second floor, and gave him a letter to take with a package to
person of rank called the lord de Montizelle, or de Monzelle, the
said respondent not knowing the name exactly and to bring the
response to the said lodging, where he was waiting for him;
adding the said respondent that having been on the rue de
Vaugirard, in the suburb of Saint Germain, across from the walls
of the Luxembourg, the said lord de Montizelle or de Monzelle,
going to the address given by master Deschauffours, he did not
find him, but spoke to a lackey dressed in gray, who told him to
leave the letter, and that his Master wold answer, that he would
take the next day to the said master Deschauffours; that not
wanting to leave the letter, nor the package, he returned to the
home of the said master Deschauffours and told him the story of
his trip; upon which the said sir master Dechauffours cried out:
"He is in quite a hurry, didn't he wait all morning!" and after the

said master Deschauffours told the said respondent he did not
think the said sir de Montizelle would keep his word, and that
consequently he must come back the next day in the morning;
that having returned the next morning to the home of the said
master Deschauffours, he similarly received from him the same
package as the day before with a letter, and returned to the home
of the said sir de Montizelle, whom he found in a morning gown,
which sir de Montizelle, after having read the letter, closely
examined the said respondent, after which he told him to wait for
the answer that he wanted to send to the said Deschauffours, and
that having written a letter, he gave it to him, telling him:
"Come, my child, I could do something for you!" that he,
respondent, having returned to the home of the said master
Deschauffours, was closely examined and questioned about his
age, what he did and what he was; that he, respondent, having
satisfied all these questions, the said master Deschauffours, told
him that the lord de Montizelle seemed to have very good
intentions toward him and he must be dressed a little more
neatly, to which the said respondent having said that he did not
have nicer clothes, the said sir Deschauffours answered that that
would be taken care of, and that he must return around eleven
thirty; that being returned around eleven thirty to the home of the
said master Deschauffours, he found there the said sir de
Montizelle, who told him that if he wanted to enter his service, to
which the said respondent said that he wanted nothing but to be
able earn his living honestly and following God, the said
Montizelle asked many more questions, and finally had him eat;
following which, after having given him forty sols, the said lord
de Montizelle told him to come back the next day and that he
wanted to dress him; that having been the next day to find the
said lord de Montizelle found in his anteroom an outfit of
drugget and linen, that having gone into the room of the said
lord, he found master Deschauffours talking with him, and that
sir de Montizelle told him to take the clothes which were in the
anteroom; that having obeyed this order, the said sir de
Montizelle told him to undress; that he not daring to undress in
front of these two Monsieurs, master Deschauffours told him:
"Come on, don't put on airs!" upon which he having obeyed, and
wanting to put on the said drugget outfit, the said master
Deschauffours had him take off his pants and his shirt, after
which the said sir de Montizelle examined him naked for a long
time, looking from time to time at master Deschauffours who
said, "Montizelle, I think what you need is right there," upon
which the said sir de Montizelle replied: "I know that." After

which the said sirs told the said respondent to take the linen and things he saw and to get dressed, which he having done, the said sir de Montizelle told him that he would take him into his service, and would give him thirty crowns a year; that at the end of two days the said master Deschauffours being come to the home of the said sir de Montizelle told the said respondent to go in, and that having closed the door of the room where they were, the said master Montizelle told him: "I haven't yet seen what this young man can do, I have to see that," that upon that the said master Deschauffours having told him respondent to approach, he took him in his arms and then undid his pants, during which time the said sir Montizelle knew him respondent carnally, despite his cries and his resistance; this being done, the said master Deschauffours told the said sir de Montizelle that he wanted his share according to his conditions, and also knew the respondent in the same way, no matter how he begged and resisted; after which the said sir de Montizelle gave him two crowns, telling him: "Don't cry, my child, I want to help you,"; that being a foreigner [*that is, from a different region*], and not knowing the consequences of what he had just done, he did not dare leave the said house, and that at the end of eight days the said sir de Montizelle having called him one evening into his room, told him that his bed was not good enough, and that he wanted to stay that night with him, which the said respondent did out of fear, the said sir de Montizelle knew him carnally three times that night; that the next day the sir de Montizelle having sent him to take a letter to the said master Deschauffours, he asked him if he was happy with his Master, and that he respondent having said yes, the master Deschauffours immediately began to try to know him carnally, which he respondent having refused, and threatened to cry out in case of violence, the said master Deschauffours answered that he wanted nothing by force; that after five or six days he, respondent, having gone to his ordinary confessor who was the the Father Anselme, a jacobin, and having faithfully told him everything that had happened to him, the said Father Anselme told him that he had committed a horrible and hateful crime, like that of the sodomites who were burned with the fire of Heaven, and if the Law knew of it he would be severely punished; that he, respondent, terrified by these words, answered Father Anselme that he had not known the consequences of what he had done; and that he had always been forced to do it; upon which the said Father Anselme told him that he should not have stayed another minute after the first violence done to him, and that he must not either take any more money, that the said respondent said about this should he denounce the said sirs Deschauffours and de Montizelle to the Law, the said Father Anselme told him no, and that sooner or later God would take vengeance on them, that perhaps the lord would have pity on him because of his innocence, and his youth, but he must as of this moment leave the said sir de Montizelle, send him back his outfit and not go there himself; and give to the poor the two crowns which he had received, and that otherwise not only would he not give him absolution, but even he would not hear him anymore, not unless he obeyed; adding the said respondent that in coming out of the confessional, having met on the rue Saint Nicolas a friend of his who was a chimney sweep, he told him to come with him to his hostess' place, where his things were, and that there having undressed and having taken again his old clothes, he gave the other things to his comrade and asked him to take them back to the said sir de Montizelle, which his said comrade having done, the sire de Montizelle had an answer sent that he would not run after the respondent of whom he was already weary; this done the said respondent gave to the poor the said two crowns that he had received from the said sir de Montizelle.

Asked if he had met anywhere the said Deschauffours, answered that he had never again seen the said sir de Montizelle, but only sometimes the said master Deschauffours, that he tried to avoid him, and acted as if he did not know him.

6th witness.

In continuing the said interrogation we had approach an individual dressed in brown and red striped cotton, called Marie Le Clerc, widow of Pierre Chaveau, hatter, who said she was thirty six, that she continued the hat business that she had when Pierre Chauveau her husband was alive, that she was from Pont de Ce in Anjou, and that she lived on the rue Granata, Saint Laurent parish.

Asked if she knew master Deschauffours, answered yes, and to her sorrow.

Asked if she knew something of the said Deschauffour's scandalous trade, and why she had said she knew him to her sorrow, answered that not knowing the foul and hateful reputation of master Deschauffours she had had the misfortune to have his business and to provide him with hats; that once having sent Armand Josse Chauveau, her oldest son, sixteen years old, and Paul Chauveau, his younger brother, fourteen years old, to the home of the said master Deschauffours to take him a beaver hat that he had had made for himself, at the time that the said master Deschauffours lived on the rue Brisemiche ["*Break loaf*"], the said master Deschauffours caressed the said Paul Chauveau a great deal and told the said Armand Josse Chauveau, that he liked the little brother, that he could go back, that the said younger would dine with him, that he would take care of him and bring him back to the said respondent after he had dined; that the said Armand Josse Chauveau suspecting nothing and regarding these demonstrations as proceeding from a real affection, returned to the said respondent, to whom he repeated what the said Deschauffours had said; which respondent not seeing the said Paul Chauveau return, went the same evening to the home of the said master Deschauffours, that she did not find him at his place, and having asked a servant of the house where the said master Deschauffours lived, if he had gone out with someone, and the said servant having answered that he was accompanied by a young boy dressed in rust, the said respondent waited for the said master Deschauffours, who did not come back until eleven at night, with the said Paul Chauveau, that having bawled out the said master Deschauffours, she took back the said Chauveau her son by force, whom she asked where he had been with the said master Deschauffours, which Paul Chauveau started to cry, and said that master Deschauffours had taken him with him to dine on the rue Montmartre, and that there there were three Monsieurs, who caressed him a great deal, and then whipped him, and put a finger in his ass, and that having wanted to ask the said master Deschauffours to defend him, instead of helping him he had done the same; adding that the said respondent not knowing what could have been done to the said Paul Chauveau her son, she examined him, and found that his behind was torn up, which made her think that her said son could have been raped by the said individuals without noticing it given his innocence; adding that after eight days the said Paul Chauveau had disappeared and did not come back to the house; that despite all the research she had been able to do to find him she had had no news for almost six years since the said Paul Chauveau got lost.

Asked when the said thing happened, answered that it was about six years before.

Asked if she had seen the said sire Deschauffours again, answered yes but that he had always denied knowing where the said Paul Chauveau was.

Asked if she had deposed a complaint for the violence committed on the said Paul Chauveau, her son, answered that Paul Chauveau her husband, then living, had prevented her.

Asked if she knew anything of the individuals who committed the said violence, answered no.

Asked if she had had any information since which makes her suspect the said Paul Chauveau had been kidnapped, answered that Jeanneton, servant of master Vitrey, *huissier à verge* [beadle, *roughly*] at the Paris Chatelet, living in the rue Brisemiche, in the same house as master Deschauffours, told him that Deschauffours was a great rascal, and that his Master had done well to have him leave his house, and that she suspected him of having kidnapped her son, but that the said Jeanneton had never wanted to say anything more.

Arrest and first interrogation

DECREE AND IMPRISONMENT OF THE SAID
DESCHAUFFOURS

At the charge of the King's Prosecutor at the Paris Chatelet we
have ordered sir Pierre Simonet, police agent, to seize the said
Benjamin Deschauffours, which done to bring the said
Deschauffours to the prisons of the Bastille in Paris, to be
questioned by ourselves, and then to be ordered as appropriate.
Done by us, Jean Baptiste Ravot, knight, lord of Ombreval,
King's Councilor in all his Councils, ordinary Master of Requests
of his house, Lieutenant General of Police of the City,
Jurisdiciton and Viscounty of Paris, this day Monday the
eighteenth day of the month of July 1725.

Commission assigned by His Majesty to sir D'Ombreval,
Lieutenant general of Paris, with power to judge conclusively
and in last resort the trial concerning Benjamin Deschauffours,
July 21, 1725. Given at Versailles, signed Louis and below
Phelippeau.

INTERROGATION OF BENJAMIN DESCHAUFFOURS in
1725.

In the years seventeen twenty five, this day Friday the twenty-
fifth day of July, we Jean Baptiste Ravot, knight of Ombreval,
asked and had brought before us an individual dressed in iron
gray cloth, presently prisoner in this castle of the Bastille, which
individual was questioned by us in the following manner:

Asked his name, answered that he was called Benjamin
Deschauffours.

Asked his age, answered that he was thirty six or thereabouts.

Asked from what region he came, answered that he was from
Viviers in Languedoc.

Asked his profession, answered that he had practiced no trade,
and lived plainly off his means.

Asked what his wealth consisted of, answered that it consisted of
annuities.

Asked who it was that paid him the said annuities, answered that
he did not want to name them.

Asked the names of his father and mother, answered that his
father was called Abraham Deschauffours and his mother bore
the name of Judith D'Artillac.

Asked the employment of the said Abraham Deschauffours,
answered that he was an officer of duties for revenues and
passage of the Rhone.

Asked if the said Abraham Deschauffours had married the said
Judith D'Artillac, answered yes.

Asked regarding the fact that there was proof to the contrary and
that the said Judith D'Artillac was only his concubine, said that
that could not be.

Asked if he knew Jean Petit, called Painque, answered yes.

Asked if he had ever had himself called Moulien Duplessis,
answered yes.

Asked for what purpose he had taken this name, answered it was
because an uncle on his mother's side bore it, and that he had just
died, and he had had an inheritance from him.

Asked what he had done with the supposed inheritance from the
so-called Moulien Duplessis, answered that he had put it into
annuities.

Asked what profession the so-called Moulien Duplessis had,
answered that he was an officer in tobacco revenue.

Asked [*sic*] that he did not speak the truth, regarding the said
Moulien Duplessis, given that making him the brother of his
mother, he had previously declared that his mother was called
Judith D'Artillac, answered that it was nonetheless true, given
that they were brother and sister of different marriages.

Asked if he had know Jean Petit, called Painque, answered that
he already been asked and that he had answered yes.

Asked how he had known the said Painque, answered that he had been in his service, and that finally the said Painque had taken his clothes and a gold watch.

Asked if he had filed any complaints and done searches regarding this, answered that he had filed no complaints, but that having fruitlessly looked for the said Painque, he was told that he had returned to his home region.

Asked what region the said Painque was from, answered that he was Burgundian.

Asked [sic] that there was proof that six years ago a lord had addressed him respondent to have a young good looking and shapely man, with whom he could commit sodomy and crimes against nature, that the respondent had provided to the said lord, which the said lord had examined naked, and had not found him to his taste, and told him in the presence of witnesses that the said boy had black skin, and badly shaped thighs and haunches, and further what is the name of the said lord and of the said boy, answered that he did not know what was being talked about.

Asked if he was not speaking the truth, given that there was also proof in the trial that being asked about this, he had answered that one should not pay attention to what the said lord said, that he was a madman and capricious, answered that he had never given that answer to anyone.

Asked why he had taken the name of marquis Du Preau, answered that it was because he wanted to buy land which bore this name.

Asked where the said land was located, said that he had never been there, and that he had been told it was in Burgundy.

Asked from whom he wanted to buy the said land, answered that he did not know the seller.

Asked the price of the said land, answered that it was offered to him at seventy thousand pounds.

Asked through whom he wanted to buy this land, answered that it was an individual named Duplain who had spoken to him of it.

Asked if he was not speaking the truth, given that it was not credible that he would have borne the name of a piece of land which he did not know, any more than the seller, and that there was proof to the contrary that he had only taken this name of Marquis Du Preau to disguise himself, answered that he had spoken the truth and that one could not prove him the contrary.

Asked that one was not obliged to prove him the contrary, although that would have been easy, but that it was up to him to prove what he claimed, answered also that he stood by what he had just said and would prove it.

Asked if he had not committed the crime of sodomy and sinned against nature with all the servants he had taken into his service, answered that he had never committed the said crime of sodomy.

Asked that he had not spoken the truth, and that to the contrary there had been too much proof to the contrary, and that, in consequence, his denial was illusory, answered that he was nonetheless ready to justify himself regarding all the accusations made against him.

Asked if among other servants who had been in his service, he had not carnally known Picard, answered that he had had several servants of this name, and he had never had any intercourse with any of them.

Asked if six to seven years ago he had involved Picard his lackey with a German lord, answered that he knew nothing of this and he had involved no one.

Asked if he had had intercourse and carnal habitation with one of his lackeys called La Fleur, answered no, and that he had never committed the said crime.

Answered if he knew the said La Fleur, answered no.

Asked that nonetheless he had just acknowledged it in denying that he had ever had any criminal intercourse with him, answered that he did not remember the said La Fleur, and he had only denied having committed the said crime of sodomy.

Asked if he knew Perron, waiter in the tavern of Buffet, wine Merchant, living on the rue des Mauvais garçons, answered no, that he had had wine at the place of the said Buffet, but he did not remember the name of any of his waiters.

Asked if that there was proof in the trial that he had wanted to force and rape the said Perron, and even that he had told him there was nothing wrong with committing the said crime, that only fools were frightened by it, answered that he knew nothing about this.

Asked that there was proof in the trial that he tried out and knew carnally all those whom he provided to different people, answered no, and he denied ever having committed the said crime in any manner.

Asked if he did not live carnally with the lackeys whom he had in his service, and if this criminal familiarity was not the reason that the said domestics took advantage of him, and only spoke to him with great insolence, answered that he had always been very good to his servants, but that only came from his natural goodness, and not because of the said crime of sodomy, which he had never committed.

Asked if he knew the individual Duplan, answered yes.

Asked who the said Duplan was, answered that he was a gentleman.

Asked that he was not saying the truth, and that there was proof that the said Duplan was only the son of a tailor, answered that the said Duplan introduced himself as a gentleman, and he had not been truly sure that he was.

Asked where the said Duplan lived, answered that he knew that he lived in the Rue du Foin, at a cobbler's, but that he did not know that it was his father.

Asked if he had not raped the said Duplan, that he then had him seduced by Picard his lackey, and then sadly abused him for a month, at the end of which time he delivered him to an English lord, who took him to live in his country, answered that he knew nothing of this, and this testimony was false.

Asked if he knew the Count de ....., answered yes. [*It is not clear whether this name was omitted in the original trial record – if this was someone important, it may have been – or if Hernandez simply could not read the name. A third, though distant, possibility is that the family name was still well-known in the early twentieth century and so he found it wisest not to include it.*]

Asked if the said Count had the same taste for sodomy, said that he knew nothing of this.

Asked if he knew M. de La Tour de Tressan, King's secretary, answered yes.

Asked if he was of the same humor and inclination, answered that he knew nothing of this.

Asked if he knew the Marquis Spinelli, a Neapolitan lord, and the Chevalier de Forbvoy, English, answered yes.

Asked if the above named were of similar humor, answered that he knew nothing of this.

Asked if he knew sir de Montizelle, answered no.

Asked if he knew sir de Monzelle, answered that he knew the Marquis de Monzelli, a Venetian lord, and the two above named.

Asked if he knew Thomas Vaupinesque, called Chambery, Savoyard by origin, answered no.

Asked if having found him one day, about three years ago, at the corner of the rue de l'Arbre sec, and having taken him to his place, and then having sent him to the home of the said sir Monzelli, with whom he came to an agreement, and sold the said Chambery, whom they raped and knew carnally the one and the other, answered that he had never seen or known the said Chambery, and that he knew nothing of this.

Asked if he knew the widow Chauveau, answered no.

Asked if he knew Paul Chaveau, answered no.

Asked that it is not enough to deny, and that there is proof in the trial that he took the said Paul Chauveau age fourteen, to the rue Montmartre, near Saint Joseph, seven years ago or thereabouts, and there raped him, as well as several other individuals who were in the said house, and who equally raped and carnally knew the said Paul Chauveau, that he respondent took him home around eleven in the evening, answered that he knew nothing of this.

Answered if at the end of eight days he kidnapped the said Paul Chauveau, answered that he does not understand.

Asked who were the three individuals who raped the said Chauveau in the said house on the rue Montmartre, answered that he had already said that he knew nothing of this.

Asked that there is proof of the above, and that there is a complaint with the commissioner of the saint Martin district where the said widow Chauveau lives, answered that he knew nothing of this complaint.

Asked the names of the three individuals above, answered that he as little knew their names as their faces.

Asked if he knew sire de Vitrey, *huissier à verge* at the Châtelet, answered no.

We told him that he was not telling the truth, given that there was too much proof that he knew him and even had stayed some time in the house of the said master Vitrey, on the rue Brisemiche, and that such things cannot be denied, answered that now he remembered.

Second group of witnesses

INQUIRY CONDUCTED BY M. RAVOT D'OMBREVAL in 1725

Today Saturday the twenty-third day of July, two o'clock in the afternoon, we questioned the following witnesses, in the following manner:

7th witness

First appeared an individual wearing a dress of siamoise, who said she was named Marie Geneviève Anquetil, that she was fifty-nine, that she was the widow of Robert Finet, master clocksmith, that she continued her said husband's business as best she could, and that she was from Paris.

Asked if she knew the said Deschauffours, answered that she knew him only too well.

Asked why she said that she only knew him too well, answered that it was because the said Deschauffours had raped and had had raped the said Hillaire Finet her son.

Asked what proof she had that the said Hillaire Finet her son had been raped, answered that Sunday the first day of this month, the said Henry Hillaire her son having gone to the home of the said sire Deschauffours to take him a watch he had had repaired, the said sire Dechauffours had had him enter, and had him drink wine in which he had apparently mixed some drug which put the said Hillaire Finet into such a sleep that he could feel that he had been known carnally and against nature; that the said sir Deschauffours, not happy with having raped him and having had him raped by two individuals who were with him, had further shamefully driven him away, and insulted him; that the said Henry Hillaire Finet, having returned to the home of the said respondent, complained of great pain in his fundament, upon which she respondent asked sir Taylor, sworn Surgeon, to examine her son, which the said sir Taylor did charitably, after which she the respondent went the next morning to M. the Commissioner de Lepinoy to file her complaint.

Asked if she knew of the scandalous dealings of the said Deschauffours, answered that she had never heard of it but that the woman Picarde, who is a *revendeuse à la toilette [an intinerant reseller of luxury items]*, could tell us quite a bit about that, having known well Duplan, who had formerly frequented the said Deschauffours, and Picard, who is from her region, and was in service with the said master, telling us to have him come and to interrogate him on these points.

8th witness.

In continuing the said interrogation we have had approach an individual dressed in mixed drugget, who said that he was called Henry Hillaire Finet, that he was sixteen and that he was a journeyman clockmaker.

Asked if he knew Deschauffours, answered yes.

Asked if he knew anything concerning the said Deschauffours, answered yes, and that first Sunday of this month the said sir Deschauffours had him eat with him and had him take some drug which put him to sleep, during which time the said sir Deschauffours and two other messieurs raped him, the respondent adding what his mother had declared at greater length... that he had nothing to add, except that he had been hurt and that he was currently sick since this incident.

9th witness.

In continuing the said interrogation we had approach an individual dressed in black cloth, who said he was called David Edward Taylor, was Irish, native of the city of Dublin, that he was forty seven, that he was of the Roman Catholic Apostolic Religion, and that having been fortunate enough to be raised in it he had always professed it.

Asked if he knew Deschauffours, answered no.

Asked if he had known that the said Deschauffours maintained a trade in sodomy, answered yes and that Sunday the first day of the present month of July, around two in the afternoon, the woman Anquetil came to ask him to come examine Henry

Hillaire Finet her son, that having gone up to the room on the
third floor at rear he saw the said Finet lying on his bed,
complaining of great pain in his fundament, that having carefully
examined the said Finet, who was hurt to the point of bleeding,
he finally recognized that the said Finet had been known
carnally; that having questioned the said Finet, he told him that
he did not know what had been done to him, giving that having
fallen asleep at the table of master Deschauffours where there were
also two individuals, he found himself alone when he awoke and
in this state; upon which he respondent asked him if he had
fallen and if he was wounded, to which the said Finet answered
no; which made the said respondent readily think that the said
Finet had been raped by Deschauffours and other individuals, but
what confirmed the said respondent in this thought, is that at the
end of eight days the said Finet's wound was not healed, which
[fact] having obliged the said respondent to examine him, he
detected a tumor on the fundament of the said Finet, upon which
not daring to be too sure about what it was, he told the said
Anquetil that he had to seek a consultation on it, at which, the
said Anquetil told him that she begged him at once to get
whatever Doctor or Surgeon he wanted, to consult on the said
wound, at which the respondent, wanting to satisfy her and with
that his professional duty, had come master Bomel, sworn
Surgeon, who examined the said Finet with the respondent, and
then prepared the written statement which the said respondent
gave us and whose sense follows.

Today Tuesday, tenth day of the month of July, we Pierre
Bomel, sworn expert Surgeon received at Saint Cosme, and
David Edward Taylor, also Surgeon, we went, etc. and after
having examined for a long time the tumor on the fundament
near the anus, recognized that the said Henry Hillaire Finet had
been known carnally and by copulation against Nature, given
that the said tumor came only from blood corrupted by a foreign
humor, and that the said tumor would without fail degenerate
into Crystalline, a disease which could only result from a
copulation in the manner said above, and which it was forbidden
to us to bandage and medicate; but given that the said widow
Finet that this interdiction could not apply in the present case,
since it was clear that the said Finet had been raped and known
carnally against Nature, it could only have been during an
involuntary sleep, and one powerful enough to keep the said
Finet from feeling any touching or violence done to him, upon
which we have prepared the current report, to use as appropriate.

Upon which we have had the said report above transcribed, the minutes of which remained with us, attached to the present official record.

10th witness.

In continuing the said interrogation we have had approach an individual dressed in redyed brown siamoise, who said she was called Jeanneton, Jeanne Trappel, that she was thirty six, and that she was a servant in the home of master Yurey, *huissier à verge* at the Chastelet.

Asked if she knew Deschauffours, answered yes.

Asked how she knew the said Deschauffours, answered that the said Deschauffours had taken an apartment in the house of the said master Vitrey. Her master, on the rue Brisemiche.

Asked if she had heard talk of the crimes and scandalous and abominable trade of the said Deschauffours, answered yes.

Asked to tell us what she knew, answered that the said master Deschauffours saw a great number of people, that one always saw new faces at his place, that young boys often went there that he whipped for his pleasure, that one often heard the said children cry, and that once she saw the said master Deschauffours returning very late one evening with a young boy of ten to eleven dressed in red, which boy was crying hot tears; that having gone up to his apartment, she heard the said boy cry even more strongly that before and say that he wanted to see his dear father and his dear mother, that the said Deschouffours answered: "Silence! Don't let me hear you anymore!" but that the said child not stopping weeping and crying the more, the said master Deschauffours apparently becoming impatient took a stick or some cane and had so struck the said boy that he wounded him on the head; that at that the said young boy, fearing that the said Deschauffours knock him out was silent, that the said Deschauffours sent a moment after his lackey to get master Vincent, surgeon, who lived on the rue de la Verrerie near des Consuls, who arriving soon after, bandaged and put the first dressing on the said young boy, and asked how the said boy could have so hurt himself, to which master Deschauffours answered that the said young boy got hurt so in fighting and kidding around with other children his age; that at that the said master Vincent said that it was a very nasty game which the said boy had played and that the blow could easily lead to death; that the said master Vincent then asked the said master Deschauffours if the boy was his, to which he answered that he was a love child; that at that the said master Vincent having left, she respondent, who had heard a part of the above, asked if the said boy was hurt to which master Vincent answered yes and even dangerously, but that nonetheless there was nothing to fear, because being a bastard, these sorts of children are never hurt; that she the respondent having said that master Deschauffours hating women too much to have bastards, the said master Vincent had answered: "He can do as he likes, it's not mine!" the said respondent adding that the said boy having fallen sick from the said blow received, and being near death, the said Deschauffours had him taken to the hotel Dieu by his lackey, where the said boy died after three days.

Asked if she had told this to Vitrey, her master, answered that she only told him when the boy was taken to the hotel Dieu, and at that the said master de Vitrey went down to the room of the said master Deschauffours, to whom he said that he absolutely did not want him living in his house anymore, and that if he did not leave within eight days, he would go file a complaint with the Commissioner.

Asked how she had known that the sad boy died at the hotel Dieu, answered that she had followed the lackey of the said Deschauffours and that she had seen him.

Asked if she had spoken to the said boy when he was put in the hotel Dieu, answered that two hours after the said boy was in the hotel dieu, he was delirious.

Asked if she had learned the name of the said boy, answered no, and that the said Deschauffours had had him put in the hotel Dieu under the name of Jasmin.

Asked if she knew the name of the said lackey of the said Deschauffours, answered yes and that he was called Picard.

Asked if she knew the names of those who frequented the house of the said Deschauffours, said that the said master Deschauffours had only lived for two and a half months in the said house of master Vitrey, and that so many people came that she could not have known them.

Asked when this incident occurred; after thinking and speaking a bit to herself, answered that it was about six years before.

Asked if she knew the widow Chauveau, answered yes, and that the said widow could give a good account of master Deschauffours' debaucheries.

Asked why she said that the said widow Chauveau could give a good account of the debaucheries of the said Deschauffours, answered that it was because the said widow had had a child kidnapped and raped by the said Deschauffours.

Asked if she knew what had happened to the said son of the sad widow Chauveau, answered that she knew nothing of it.

Asked what proof she had that it was the said Deschauffours who had kidnapped the said Chauveau, answered that it is because one day she heard the said Picard the lackey of the said master Deschauffours, who did not think anyone heard, say to his Master that the Hatter's son was quite far away, and that he had no reason to worry about him.

Asked when the said Picard had said that, answered that it was about a month after the said master Deschauffours had taken the said Chauveau to dine.

11th witness.

In continuing the said interrogation we have had approach an individual in a brown outfit, wearing a bonnet wig. Who said he was called Augustin Caperal, called Languedoc, that he was from Carcassonne in Languedoc, that he was twenty-eight and that he was a journeyman with master Gillet, merchant Apothecary in Paris, living there on the rue des Lombards.

Asked if he knew Deschauffours, answered yes, and that one day the said master Deschauffours having come to the place of sir Gillet, his Master, to get ointment, that the said master Gillet not then being in the shop, he respondent asked master Deschauffours what sort of ointment he wanted, that the said master Deschauffours having asked for ointment to stop the bleeding of a wound, he answered that there were different ointments depending on the wounds, and that he had only to show him the prescription from the Doctor or Surgeon, that he had in the shop all the different drugs one could want; upon which the said Deschauffours told the said respondent that he begged him to bring several drugs with him, and that he would see what sort was required; at which he respondent having taken two or three of the most common drugs for these sorts of matters, he followed the said master Deschauffours, who took him to a house on the rue Saint Martin, near Saint Julien des Menestriers, where having gone up to the second floor he found a young man lying on a bed, the said young man very pale and run down; that the said Deschauffours told him to be discreet and he would pay him well, that having taken off the covers from the bed where the young man was lying, which done he saw that the said young man was covered with blood he had lost, because he had just been completely castrated; that he respondent cried out at this, and that the said Deschauffours told him to say nothing and to try to remedy this; that he respondent having said that he found it quite extraordinary that he had been brought, the said Deschauffours answered that this was a man whose parts had become so gangrenous that it was necessary to cut them off; that at this he respondent said that the Surgeon who had done this operation should have put the first dressing on it; but that during this time the patient on the bed having fainted, he thought he must provide the promptest remedy he could, while an individual that master Deschauffours called his Lackey and that he named Picard brought the young man back around; that that being done the said master Deschauffours wanted to give the said respondent a louis which he refused, and said that it was only thirty five sols; that on that the said master Deschauffours asked the said respondent to keep this matter secret, given that this young man was about to get married, adding the said individual that having left the said House he returned to that of master Gillet, his Master, to whom he thought he must tell what had just happened.

Asked if he had not learned the name of the young man so castrated, answered yes, that the hostess of the said House at whom the said master Gillet had advised him to inquire had answered yes, that this young man was an Italian native of Modena, named Bizetti.

Asked if he had learned anything more, answered that the said hostess had further told him that he was the son of an Italian actor, that he had been sent to France because he seemed to have a beautiful face, and in fact came to be castrated.

INTERROGATIONS OF TUESDAY July 26, 1725.

12th Witness.

Firstly appeared an individual wearing a dress of black etamine, who said that she was called Michelle Claudine Polet, that she was fifty six, that she was a *revendeuse à la toilette*, answered weeping that she was a widow, that her husband was called Jean Barbet, that he was a servant in the house of Monsieur the Count de Tonnerre.

Asked why she had wept in naming her said husband answered that it was only eighteen months since he had died, and that she could not keep from crying when she thought of him.

Asked why she could not keep from crying and if her husband had met some unhappy end, answered no, and that it was only from the love they had for each other.

Upon which we have told her that the said Jean Barbet was quite worthy of praise, and then we asked her what region she was from, she answered that she was from Amiens.

Asked if she had known master Deschauffours, answered yes, and that she had sold him many things, and bought others, and had lent him several times money in pawn and without interest.

Asked if she knew anything of the infamous and scandalous doings of the said Deschauffours, answered yes and that beyond what she knew of it, she had learned much more from Picard, lackey of the said master Deschauffours, and from big Jeanne, servant of the widow Doreau, mistress of a rooming house where the said master Deschauffours had lived some time; that the said master Deschauffours had changed names several times and went by that of Moulien Duplessis, at the time that he lived on the rue des Bons enfans, that of Desfourneaux, about four years ago, and when he lived on the vieille rue du Temple, and also that during a certain time, and notably while he lived on the rue Poupée, at the home of the said widow Doreau, the name of Marquis du Préau.

Asked to tell us about the circumstances of which she had
knowledge, answered that she had known Joseph Duplan, who
was the son of a tailor who lived on the rue du Foin facing the
Mathurins, which Duplan being taken one day to the home of the
said master Deschauffours by the said Picard his lackey, had
been known carnally by the said Deschauffours, and that having
felt a great deal of pain from this embrace, he had struck the said
master Deschauffours, and having gone out brusquely from his
house saying that he had been deceived, that he did not think that
would hurt so much; that nonetheless a few days later Picard
having encountered him and asking him how he was, the said
Duplan answered that his pain had quickly passed; upon which
the said Picard replied that there were ointments to give relief,
and that all he had to do was to come to his Master's place, that
that would make him happy; that at that the said Duplan having
come to the house of the said master Deschauffours, had criminal
intercourse with him for almost a month, urging the said master
Deschauffours all the while to find him some lord he could be
with, and that finally the said master Deschauffours had found an
English lord whose name she, respondent, did not know, who
gave a regular pension to the said Duplan, and took him to his
country.

Asked if she knew that master Deschauffours abused all his
domestics, and tried out all those whom he supplied and sold to
the one and the other, answered yes and that the said Picard had
admitted that to her, and that he was quite weary of putting up
with the said Deschauffours' carnal copulation; but that he was
repaid in obliging master Deschauffours to allow him carnal
relations with those who came to the said house.

Asked if she knew of other matters, answered that there was a
young man with blond hair, and always wore red heels, which
young man was loved by master Deschauffours, who did not
introduce him to anyone, and who came every evening when
there was no one there; that nonetheless the said Picard had
obliged the said master Deschauffours to allow him to sleep with
the said young man, which he had a great deal of trouble
achieving.

*[Red heels were typically a sign of nobility, but appeared to be
an ostentation in this case.]*

Asked how she knew all that, answered that she had heard it from the said Picard.

Asked why the said Picard told her such things, which were not to his credit, answered that the said Picard did not think he was doing anything wrong, and besides she had made him admit everything at the time that the said Picard was thinking of leaving this shameful business, and that she respondent wanted to marry him [!], which did not prove possible.

Asked if she knew where the said Picard is answered no.

Asked if she had known some of the people who frequented the house of the said Deschauffours, answered that she had seen there M. the Count de Kabia and Monsieur the Marquis de Sautereau, Monsieur the Marquis Spinelli, a rich Italian lord, and Monsieur the Chevalier Forbvoy an English Milord, and that she had known from the said Picard that the said master Deschauffours had finally sold and delivered to maser Chevalier Forbvoy the said blond boy mentioned above, and whose name she does not know, the said Picard never having wanted to tell it to her, except that said he was the son of a lawyer; adding that the said master Deschauffours had sold another boy to the said Marquis Spinelli when he returned to his country.

13th Witness.

In continuing the interrogation we had approach an individual dressed in black cloth, who answered that he was called Georges Vincent, that he was forty two and that he was a sworn Surgeon received at Saint Cosme.

Asked if he knew Deschauffours, answered yes.

Asked how he knew him, answered that he had seen him only once.

Asked if he knew that the said Deschauffours maintained a trade of sodomy, answered that many people had told him so.

Answered when he had seen the said Deschauffours, answered that one evening around eleven, a lackey came to knock at his

door on the rue de la Verrerie and told him to come care for a
young man who had cracked his head; that having followed the
said lackey he went into a room on the first floor of a house on
the rue Brisemiche, where he found a young child of ten to
eleven years old, who had his head broken, as it seemed to us
[*sic*], by a blow of a stick, which boy did not talk while he
respondent tended to him and applied the first dressing, and it
even seemed to the respondent that, either naturally or otherwise,
the said boy was a little slow; that having asked master
Deschauffours, who was the Master of the apartment, how the
said boy had hurt himself so, the said master Deschauffours
answered that it was in fighting and fooling around with friends,
and that the said boy was a little rascal and a wretch, who did not
deserve the bread he gave him; adding the said respondent that
he had told the said master Deschauffours that this wound
seeming to him freshly made, he was surprised given the hour
that the said boy was still playing and fooling around in the
streets, at which the said master Deschauffours had answered
shortly: "Monsieur, it's not so complicated! See if you want to
treat him or no, and I will go find another Surgeon." That he
respondent, more concerned with the young boy's state than with
the discourse of the said master Deschauffours, continued to treat
the said young boy and recognized that his wound was quite
dangerous and even mortal, that he told the said master
Deschauffours, who seemed to be and claimed to be his father, at
which the said Deschauffours said: "So much the better, that will
be one bastard the less in the world! There are enough whores in
Paris to replace him!" [*Ironically, we later learn that
Deschauffours himself was born out of wedlock.*] After which the
said respondent asked the said master Deschauffours if he
wanted him to come back the next day to examine the said boy,
to which the said master answered no, and gave him forty sols,
after which he left the said house.

Asked if he knew the name of the said boy, answered no.

Asked if he knew the name of the lackey of the said
Deschauffours, answered yes, and that he had heard him called
Picard.

Asked when the said thing happened, answered that it was about
six or seven years ago.

14th Witness.

In continuing this interrogation we had approach an individual dressed in brown cloth, with buttons, button holes and silver galloons on the said outfit, and carrying a sword, who told us he was called Ambroise Corne Vitrey, that he was sixty-seven, and that he was *huissier à verge* at the Paris Châtelet and that he lived in a house that belonged to him respondent on the rue Brisemiche.

Asked if he knew Deschauffours answered yes.

Answered if he knew that the said Deschauffours maintained a bad trade, and committed and had committed the crime of sodomy, kidnapped children to sell them, and other such crimes, answered that he had heard talk of this, that the said Deschauffours had rented an apartment in his house and that many people came there whom he did not know.

Asked if the said Deschauffours had stayed a long time in the said house, answered that he had only lived there three months, given that during this time the said master Deschauffours had brought to his place an unknown young boy and whose name he does not know, and had cracked his head with a stick; that Jeanneton, his servant, who had heard the whole thing, and who told him that the said master Deschauffours had sent the said boy to the hôtel Dieu, where he died after three days, told him of this, upon which he, respondent, had gone the first thing in the morning to tell master Deschauffours that he absolutely wanted him out within eight days, otherwise he would go file a complaint with a Commissioner; that at that the said Deschauffours had said that he agreed to leave on the eighth of the following month, which he did.

Asked if he knew the lackey of the said Deschauffours, answered yes, and that he had heard him called Picard.

15th Witness

In continuing this interrogation we had approach an individual wearing a red and white striped satin Dress, who said she was called Barbe Chappey, that she was thirty eight, that she was married to Laurent Le Franc, brandy merchant and distiller in Paris.

Asked if she rented furnished rooms, answered yes, but that she has her book signed by Monsieur the Commissioner Regnard.

Asked if she knew Deschauffours, answered yes and that he had lodged at her place.

Asked if she knew of the said Deschauffours' bad trade, answered yes, and that she had heard it talked about. Asked if she knew of some circumstances around it, answered that she had seen coming and going from the home of the said master Deschauffours several men of all kinds and that also quite often men in livery and quite magnificent came there, but that she had seen nothing which could have proved the filthy trade of the said master Deschauffours, who from what everybody said trafficked in sodomy and sins against nature, that she had only seen come to the house of the said master Deschauffours a young man dressed in red camlet, who slept with him and did not come out; that the next day, around two in the afternoon, she saw go in an individual whom she did know, which individual was dressed in drugget, whom she had quietly followed and went into a Study near the Bedroom of the said master Deschauffours, that she had heard when the said individual went in, the said master Deschauffours told him: "We've been waiting for you for quite a while", at which the said individual said that he could not come earlier; that at that the young man dressed in red had said: "At least, don't make me suffer!" That on that the said person dressed in drugget said that he was going to dispatch him quickly, at which master Deschauffours added: "Have no fear, Monsieur Bizetti, you are in the hands of a skilled man", that after she heard the said young man dressed in red cry out a great deal; that the said master Deschauffours said: "One must suffer a little, but you are going to trade something you can do without for a beautiful voice", which the said respondent listening more carefully and going up to a false door which gave onto the said room, heard the said master Deschauffours speaking softly with the said young man in red, and that after she heard loud cries, and the said master Deschauffours who said: "It's done!" That during this time there was a noise in the stairs, at which noise the man dressed in drugget panicked and fled, that master Deschauffours not having been able to retain him, the said young man in red said: "Monsieur Deschauffours, I beg you not to let me perish", at which the said master Deschauffours answered: "Monsieur Bizetti, I am going to bind you with an old cravat", which he then did and then went out to find an apothecary, and came back some times later with a young man who not knowing what was going on nonetheless helped the said Bizetti, which Bizetti was over eight days without leaving his bed and without appearing.

Asked why she did not go file a complaint with the Commissioner of what she had just heard, answered that the lackey of the said master Deschauffours had led her to understand that this young man had had himself castrated because his parts were spoiled, and it was feared that gangrene set in.

Asked if she knew the name of the said lackey, answered yes, and that he was called Picard.

Asked if she knew the name of the said individual above, who was dressed in drugget and who performed this performed this operation, answered no, but that she had heard from the said master Deschauffours that he was the son of a surgeon.

16th Witness.

In continuing this interrogation we had approach an individual dressed in brown cloth and carrying a cane, who told us he was called Laurent Le Franc, that he was Picard, native of Abbeville, that he was forty five, that he was a brandy merchant-distiller and that his wife rented furnished rooms.

Asked if he knew Deschauffours, answered yes.

Asked if he knew the scandalous dealings of the said Deschauffours; answered that the rumor was common in his neighborhood, and that it was said that the said master trafficked in sodomy.

Asked if he had known anything on his own, answered no, but that his wife told him that the young boy in red who came to stay with the said master Deschauffours had been entirely castrated, and that it was the said master Deschauffours who had had this operation done.

Asked if he knew the young man dressed in red, said that he had never seen him.

Asked if he knew anything else of the said Deschauffours, answered that he only concerned himself with his shop and that it was his wife who looked after the said furnished rooms, and in consequence he had little seen and never frequented the said master Deschauffours.

Continuation of the inquiry done in 1725

INTERROGATIONS OF FRIDAY AUGUST 3.

17th Witness.

And firstly appeared before us an individual dressed in gray white cloth, with black and white galloons, who said he was named Pierre Guillois, called Champagne, that he was thirty six, that he was from Aumalle, and that he was foot servant to Monsieur the Duke de Bouillon.

Asked if he knew Deschauffours, answered no, but that four months ago an individual dressed in a red cloak had kidnapped his, the respondent's, son, only seven years old, which child was with him, respondent, and his mother; that he, respondent, having run after the said individual lost him in the crowd and he learned through Botel, Domestic of Monsieur the Duke d'Antin, that the said individual, whom he had seen pass by, was called Deschauffours; at which he, respondent, had at once gone to a Commissioner to bring a complaint.

Asked with which Commissioner he had brought his complaint, answered that it was with the Commissioner Labbé.

18th Witness.

In continuing this interrogation, we had approach an individual wearing a dress of redyed yellow satin, who said she was called Marguerite La Plaine, that she was thirty six, that she was from Paris, that she was a reseller and married to Pierre Guillois, called Champagne.

Asked if she knew Deschauffours, answered no, but that about four months ago Jullien Guillois, son of her the respondent, and of the said Pierre Guillois, had been kidnapped on the rue du faubourg Saint Antoine, and that she had been told it was the said Master Deschauffours who had done it.

Here follows the sense of the complaint lodged by the said Guillois and his wife before Master Labbé.

In the year seventeen hundred twenty five, today Sunday the ninth day of the month of April, in the presence of ourselves, Philippe Labbé, King's Counselor, Commissioner at the Chatelet, investigator assigned to the Police in the saint Antoine district, appeared Pierre Guillois and Marguerite La Plaine, his wife, and also Adrien Boutel, who complained to us that on this day, around seven in the evening, while returning from the Parc de Vincennes, with Jullien Guillois, their son of seven, they saw an individual covered in a scarlet cloak, which individual kidnapped the said Julien Guillois and ran away through the crowd, so that the said Guillois and his wife could not reach or recognize him, adding the said complainants also present before us had seen the said individual, whom he had recognized as Master Deschauffours, of which he had informed the said Guillois and his wife; as the said Boutel currently also declares, confirming as true that it is the said Master Deschauffours who committed the said kidnapping.

19ᵗʰ Witness.

In continuing the said interrogation, we have had approach an individual dressed in gray camlet, who said he is named Adrien Boutel, called L'Olive, that he was forty, that he was a servant of Monsieur the Duc d'Antin, and that he was from Nantes in Brittany.

Asked if he knew Deschauffours, answered that he knew him by sight.

Asked if he knew of the scandalous traffic of the said Deschauffours, answered that he knew of it, having heard it spoken of.

Asked if he knew any details, answered no, only that about four months ago in returning from a Sunday walk in the evening, he saw the said Deschauffours holding a child wrapped in a scarlet cloak, and that he only saw the feet of the said child; that a moment after he had seen Guillois and his wife who complained that an individual covered by a red cloak had just kidnapped their son; at which he, respondent, told the said Guillois and his wife that he had just seen pass the said kidnapper who was Master Deschauffours, but that having looked for him in vain, he, respondent, had advised the said Guillois and his wife to go file a complaint with a Commissioner, which complaint he had also filed with them the same evening with master Commissioner Labbé, who lived on the rue Saint Antoine by the hôtel de Sully [*today at 62, rue Saint-Antoine, and the headquarters of the* Caisse Nationale des Monuments Historiques et des Sites].

20th and last Witness.

In continuing this interrogation we have had come an individual dressed in black cloth, who said that he was named Jérôme Jourdain, that he was from Paris, that he was a merchant apothecary, and that he was forty nine.

Asked if he knew Deschauffours, answered no, but that one day an individual dressed in cinder gray camlet came into his shop on the rue vieille du Temple, near the rue des Blancs Manteaux, and asked him for ointments and drugs for softening and easing the fundament; that he, respondent, gave him an ointment that he thought most appropriate for that, and when he left, Grandon, son of him respondent, strongly rebuked him, and said that the said individual had a bad reputation everywhere for the crime of sodomy, and that in a word, it was master Deschauffours.

[*The following appears here, though apparently out of order:*]

March 20, 1726, a Commission was assigned by His Majesty to master Hérault, Lieutenant General of Police, carrying the power to judge without appeal the criminal trial of Benjamin Deschauffours. Inserted in the Registers of the King's State Council, signed Louis, and below Phelippeaux.

This decision says: "..And as we have had need of the said lord D'Ombreval whom we have named our intendant in the generality of Tours... »

Second interrogation of Deschauffours

INTERROGATION OF BENJAMIN DESCHAUFFOURS IN
1726.

[HERNANDEZ NOTES: *"This interrogation in large part
reproduces that preceding, and so we will limit ourselves to
reproducing those which present some difference."*]

Today Monday, fifth day of the month of April, at seven in the
morning, we, René Hérault, Knight Lord of Fontaine, Labbé,
King's Councilor in all his Councils, ordinary Master of Requests
of his hotel, Lieutenant General of Police in this City,
jurisdiction and viscomty of Paris have ordered and had brought
before us an individual dressed in iron gray cloth, etc.

Asked from what region he came, answered that he was from
Viviers in Vivarets.

We told him there was proof to the contrary of what he said, that
his father and mother were married, given that the said Abraham
Deschauffours was married, and that the said Judith D'Artillac
died before the wife of the said Deschauffours, and so the said
Judith D'Artillac could only have been his concubine, he said
that was not true.

Asked in what the supposed inheritance of Moulien Duplessis
consisted, answered that it consisted of stock in the Company of
the Indes, which he the respondent had sold and converted to a
regular pension.

Asked on what side the said Moulien Duplessis was his uncle,
answered that he was the brother of Abraham Deschauffours'
mother.

Asked [sic] that he was not speaking the truth, given that he had
previously said that the said Moulien Duplessis was the half-
brother by her mother of the said Judith D'Artillac, answered that
he was mistaken and that what he said now was the truth.

Asked where is the said land of the Preau, answered that he had never seen it and that he only knew it was in upper Burgundy.

Asked the price of the said land, answered that it was being sold to him for sixty thousand livres.

Asked that he was not saying the truth, given that he had previously said it was previously being offered to him at seventy thousand livres, and that besides his tale is badly imagined and unbelievable, and that besides that there is proof in the trial that he only took the name the Marquis de Preau to disguise himself and to fool someone, he answered that he had told the truth.

Asked that it was proved in the said trial that he, respondent, was known all over Paris as a man who ran a business in sodomy, answered he had never heard that.

Upon which we told that he was a great rascal and a great wretch, and that there was too much proof for his denials to do him any good.

Asked that there was proof in the trial that he had furnished young boys to the said Chevalier de Forbwy and Marquis Spinelli, answered that he had never been involved with supplying boys to them, nor to anyone else.

Asked if he knew what had become of the said de Monzelli, answered that the said Marquis returned long ago to Venice, and that he had heard he was dead.

Asked that there was proof and enough witnesses in the trial that he had supplied the said Chambery to the said Marquis de Monzelli, and that they had both known him carnally, answered that he knew nothing of this, and that he had never seen the said Chambery, who is apparently a false witness.

Asked if he had not held the said Chambery in his arms while the said Monzelli committed the crime of sodomy with him, and that when the said Monzelli had committed the said crime, he respondent had not told the said Monzelli that by his standard practice he should have his part in the pleasure, and even that he should have gone first, and that after while the said Monzelli held the said Chambery, he respondent knew the said Chambery, he said that he knew nothing of this, and that this accusation is as false as that above.

Upon which was showed him a memoir containing a merchant's bill for hats to the said respondent at the bottom of which was a balance with a signature in the hand of the said respondent and signed Deschauffours, and asked the said respondent if he knew this writing, who said yes, at which we told him that he was a great scoundrel and a knave to deny having ever known the said Chauveau while he still owed her seventy eight livres mentioned in the above balance, at which the said respondent said that he knew the said Chauveau well and that he recalled her, but he knew neither the said Chauveau her son nor any of the above.

Asked if he knew the said Henry Hillaire Finet, answered yes and a moment later said he did not know the said Finet.

Asked that there was proof in the trial that Sunday the second day of July 1725, the said Finet having come to bring him work that had been done, he, respondent, had the table set and had him take something in wine, which put the said Finet to sleep, so that during his sleep he, respondent, and two other individuals of which one was dressed in ras de Saint Maure, and the other in brown silk stuff, had carnally known and raped the said Finet, answered that he knew nothing of this.

Asked the names of the said individuals, answered that he knew nothing of this.

Asked which of the two was sickly and had blood so spoiled that from the said violence the said Finet got sick with chrystaline, answered that he knew nothing of this and that he does not know the names and the effects of this illness.

Asked that his denial was pointless, given that there more than enough witnesses and proofs to convict him of this deed, answered that it was impossible.

Asked what was the name of the young man whom he had kidnapped about seven years ago from his father and mother's, and taken to his place in the rue Brisemiche where he lived, and that the said child protesting, he, respondent, had beaten him so badly with a stick that he had cracked his head, so that he was obliged to go find a surgeon to see to him, he answered that he had indeed lived on the rue Brisemiche at the home of Vitrey, who is a *huissier*, but that the above never happened to him, and that he does not know what is being talked about, and that it is apparently as false and insulting an accusation as those preceding.

Asked if he had not told the Surgeon who had seen to the said child that the said child was a bastard of his, the respondent's, answered that he did not understand.

Asked if it was not true that Picard, valet to him, the respondent, had taken the said young child to the hôtel Dieu, answered that he knew nothing of this.

Asked that there was proof and witnesses in the current trial that he, respondent, living on the rue Saint Martin, had one day had castrated an individual who was at his place for two days, answered that this was as false as the above.

Answered the name of the said individual, answered that he knew nothing of this.

Asked on what occasion and for what purpose he had the said individual castrated, answered that he had already said he knew nothing of this and that he knows no more.

Asked if he had not been to the rue des Lombards, to the place of master Gillet, merchant apothecary, from where he brought a journeyman of the said master Gillet to bandage and staunch the bleeding from the wound of the said individual, answered that he does not know what is meant.

Asked if he had not told the said journeyman apothecary that the said individual had been dangerously wounded in his secret parts, so that fearing that gangrene set in it was necessary to perform an amputation, answered that he knows no more than as above.

Asked if he knew the name of the journeyman apothecary who
came to bandage the said individual, answered that he does not
know what is being talked about.

Asked if he knew the name of the individual dressed in drugget
who had performed the said operation, answered as well that he
did not know what was being talked about.

Asked if he knew Duplan, answered no.

Asked that he was not telling the truth, and that he had just
admitted above having known the said Duplan, answered that he
could never have said that he knew the said Duplan, given that it
was quite true that he did not know him in any way, unless this
individual had another name than Duplan, and by which name
he, respondent, might have known him, at which we showed him
the present trial record and showed him on it where he admitted
[knowing] the said Duplan.

Asked if he knew the widow Barbet, called La Picarde, answered
yes, by the signs of the said La Picarde being a great thief, and a
swindler, who lent on pawn, but almost never returned the
objects pawned, adding the said respondent that the said Picarde
was in love with Picard, lackey to him the respondent, and that
she gave the said Picard everything she could earn, or rather
steal, so he would sleep with her, and that besides the said
Picarde was a madame, and had provided whores to the said
Picard, upon which one day they agreed that she the said Picarde
would bring streetwalkers to the said Picard every time she
wanted to sleep with him, which whores were paid and brought
at the said Picarde's expense.

Asked how he knew these things, he answered that one day he
had reproached the said Picard, saying that he was quite foolish
to amuse himself with an old Cadaver like the said Picarde, to
which the said Picard answered that this old bird provided him
with money and girls, and that was the source of his tolerance for
her and that the said Picard had added that he made her wait
quite a while, and made her beg him to sleep with her, but that
the said Picarde was so in love with him that she submitted to
whatever he wanted.

Asked the name of the individual to whom he, respondent, had sold and provided the said Duplan, answered that it was quite true that he knew the said Duplan, but that he had never sold or provided him to anyone, and that he had never sold or provided anyone, and that because he did not like women everyone spread the rumor that he liked boys, but that that was false, very false.

At which we told him he was not telling the truth, he admitting presently that everyone knew him for a sodomite, and that he having previously denied that he knew he had this reputation, at which he answered that he had never thought that he had this reputation, but what he was talking about was the false accusations that had been made against him before us, and that it was his enemies who had lied so.

Asked if it was not true that he had promised the said Picard his valet to know carnally all those who frequented his house, answered that he knew nothing of this.

Asked the name of the English lord to whom he had sold the said Duplan, answered that we had already asked him this question and that he had answered that he had never had been in such a business.

Asked that there was proof and witnesses that he had sold and provided to the said chevalier Forbwy a young individual a young man with blond hair, and that he, respondent, had for a long time known carnally, answered that he did not know what we were talking about.

Asked the name of the young man whose head he had cracked, and that he had then sent to the Hotel Dieu, answered that he knew nothing of this.

Asked if it was not true that he had had him put in the hôtel Dieu under the name of Jasmin, answered that he knew nothing of this.

Asked that there were witnesses that the said individual whom he had had castrated was dressed in red camlet, answered that he knew nothing of this.

Asked the name of the said individual, said that he could not say anything else than as above.

Asked that there were witnesses who depose that he, respondent, present at the operation of the said individual dressed in red, and the said individual not being too resolved to suffer, he, respondent, had said in these very words: "You're making a big deal over a few nasty shreds that you are going to trade for a beautiful voice, and you will have the further advantage of not worrying about women!" that the said individual had answered that one must not joke about such serious conjectures, answered that he did not know what we were talking about.

Asked if it was not true that the said individual had had himself castrated to have a nice voice, answered that he knew nothing of this.

Asked the name of the individual who had performed the said operation, answered as well that he did not know what we meant.

Asked if it is not true that the said thing was done two years ago, answered two years ago that he, respondent, lived on the rue Saint Martin, but otherwise he did not know what we meant.

At which we told him that the said individual had made so much noise during the said operation that the whole quarter knew of it, and that several witnesses had deposed against him, he answered that even if the whole Saint Martin district testified against him that could only be false testimony, and that he repeated again that he had always told us the truth.

Asked what he had done with the young boy of seven that he had kidnapped on the grand rue du faubourg Saint Antoine, Sunday, April 9, 1725, answered that he knew nothing of this and that he had never so much as thought of kidnapping children.

Asked that there were witnesses who deposed that they had seen him do this thing, and that he then had a great scarlet cloak, under which he had hidden the said child, answered that he did not know what we were speaking of, that he had been a few times to the Saint Antoine suburb, that in his life he had worn several red cloaks, but that he had never committed the crime that these false witnesses imputed to him, and that he even remembered that this day was a very nice one, and that he, respondent, was then near Orléans on a property belonging to one of his friends.

Asked the name of this friend owner of the said property near Orléans, refused to tell it.

Asked the name of the said property, refused to tell it.

Upon which we pointed out to him that these refusals proved his crime as much as the testimony and public declarations that had been made against him.

Asked where was Paul Chauveau whom he had admitted having kidnapped, answered that he could not have admitted that he had kidnapped the said Paul Chauveau since it was not true, and he denied having ever said that.

Asked why the individual dressed in drugget, who had performed the operation on the individual whom he, respondent, had admitted was called Bizetti, had fled and had left the said operation imperfect and the said Bizetti losing blood, answered that he had never admitted having known the said Bizetti, that he did not know him at all, any more than the said individual dressed in drugget.

Asked if he had not had the illness chrystaline, answered that he knows nothing of this illness.

Asked if the said illness was common among those who committed the said crime of sodomy and sinned against nature, he answered that even were that so, he could not have been subject to the said illness, having never committed the said crime of sodomy and sins against Nature.

We pointed out to him that despite all the denials he had just made on every charge against him, and of which there were sufficient witnesses for each, he had also very often changed his tale and had varied in his responses, to which he answered us that he may have made mistakes, but that in his last answers he had told the truth, and that he was ready to undergo a second examination, at which we told him we were going to have him read the present written record, and that if he wanted to add something he could.

After which reading, the respondent having declared that he had only spoken the truth and that if he had made a few mistakes he stood by his last answers.

Re-interviews of witnesses

Although this inquiry was held by a special commission, this step and the next one were standard in the very bureaucratic progress of Old Regime justice, in which the witnesses were asked to confirm their statements and then to repeat their testimony in front of the accused.

INQUIRY CONDUCTED IN 1726

DEPOSITIONS OF TUESDAY APRIL 13

[HERNANDEZ NOTES: *"The following witnesses being the same as in the first inquiry, we will limit ourselves to enumerating them, and to only note the variations between their declarations and the preceding ones."* However, in some cases the following seems to repeat what has already been said above.]

1st Witness.

Jean Petit, called Painque.

First went into service with master Tourton, banker, rue Quincquempoix [*Quincampoix*] and then was in that of master Deschauffours, then living on the rue des Bons enfans, near the door of the Kitchen Courtyard [*la Cour des Cuisines*] of the Palais Royal... at the death of which master de Boisauvert, he remained without employment until the twenty third day of last March, when he went into service with master Moullard, horse dealer.

2nd Witness.

We had approach an individual dressed in brown cloth, with a jacket of gray linen and a sword, who said he was named Regnault Poitret, that he had enlisted in the gardes françoises regiment, but that he had resigned and obtained his leave six weeks ago...

Asked if he knew that the said La Fleur had had any bad
intercourse with the said Deschauffours, answered that he was
entirely unaware of it, given the little time he had stayed at
Deschauffours', having only stayed there a month.

3rd Witness.

We had approach an individual dressed in hazelnut colored
camlet and carrying a cane, named Arnaud Daniel Perron....

At which the said master Dechauffours replied to him that he
knew a good way to bring him satisfaction and money, with
running the risk of catching any diseases, as could happen if he
frequented whores, and that he wanted to introduce him to a lord
of the best sort, who had seen him and loved him madly, to
which the said respondent answered that besides the fact that
such a friendship was not to his taste, it made him run the risk of
being burned, which is much greater and more shameful than
losing one's money.

4th Witness.

Jeanne Elisabeth, called La Grande Jeanne.....

And that besides the said Marquis Du Preau was a nasty man and
known in the neighborhood as a foul individual who slept with
boys and hated women and girls with all his heart and had come
to his place beggars and chimney sweeps, so long as they were
good looking, which chimney sweets he had washed and
scrubbed, and then had them sleep with him after having given
them a good supper; that she often saw people of that sort there;
that the said Marquis also slept with and carnally lived with his
lackeys, and above all with Picard, which is why too all the
lackeys, in particular the said Picard, were insolent and had
themselves dressed almost as well as the said Marquis; that very
fine gentlemen also came there often and passed entire after-
dinners and even sometimes stayed the night, that the said Picard
was used to that, and had the said persons use a hidden stairs,
and that above all she saw come a young blond dressed in gray
white, and who always wore red heels, whose name she no
longer recalls, went almost every evening to the said Marquis'
place, above all when there was company....

....At which the said Picard answered: "Come, come! Let's drink one just the same, our Master and those with him have quite other things to do than to send you on an errand; they can't quit each other, and all have each other threaded by the ass like maybugs!" and that at that the said La Fleur answered: "There's some nasty B******** and I think I will soon stick them there!"...

Asked where she had learned the name of the said Duplan, answered that having followed him one evening, she saw him go into the said rue du Foin, into a little door facing the wall of the Mathurins, and that having asked in a cobbler's shop below if he knew the said young man, she was told yes, and that this young man was the son of a tailor who lived in the house and who was named Duplan...

Asked if she knew where the said Dubois was at present, answered no, and that she nonetheless thought he was still in service in Paris, and had even heard that he was somewhere in the Marais.

Asked if she had not alerted the widow Doreau, her mistress, of the bad dealings of the said supposed Marquis answered yes, and that she was the reason that the said widow Doreau had had him leave her place, preferring to lose almost six hundred livres which the said Marquis owed her than to put up with him any longer....

Asked if she had also warned the said Duplan, tailor, of his son's bad behavior, answered that having gone one way to the home of the said Duplan and having told him what she knew, the said Duplan told her that she was quite insolent, and he trusted his son for whom he would answer with his very body, and had even wanted to strike the said respondent.

5*th* *Witness.*

Thomas Vaupinesque, called Chambery.

Answered that he was a dock hand and scrubbed shoes at the Palais Royal square.

6th Witness.

We had approach an individual wearing a satin dress with red
and white stripes, who said she was called Marie Le Clerc
widow Chauveau, and lived on the rue Darnetal, in the Saint
Laurent parish, facing the *Chariot d'or*....

That on that she had been the next day to the home of the said
master Deschauffours to rebuke him strongly for what had
happened, asking him the names of those to whose home he had
taken the said Paul Chauveau, at which the said master
Deschauffours answered that he had no idea what she was
talking about, and that the said Paul Chauveau had not been
mistreated at all, and that the said individuals were people from
the Countryside who were to leave the said morning to return to
Languedoc where they were from, that having not been able to
get any better information from him, she had returned home.....

Asked if she had been able to find the said individuals who lived
on the rue Montmartre, answered that she went there with the
said Paul Chauveau, but that he could never recognize the place
where the said master Deschauffours had taken him.....

Asked what reason the said Pierre Chauveau could have for
preventing the said complaint, answered that her said husband
had implied that perhaps she was wrong and that at worst he
could find nothing out, and that this incident would reflect badly
on them.

7th Witness.

We had approach an individual wearing a dress of brown
etamine, who said she was called Marie Geneviève Anquetil, the
widow Finet.

8th Witness.

Henri Hillaire Finet.

9th Witness.

David Edward Taylor, surgeon.

10th Witness.

We had approach an individual dressed in white linen, who said she was named Jeanne Trappel, called Jeanneton....

Asked why she had been slow to alert the said Vitrey, her master, answered that she did not dare to speak to him of it.

Asked why she did not dare to speak to him of it, answered that she thought the said boy was a relation of the said master Deschauffours, so that he was free to treat him as he wished.

At which we told her that even if that was true, fathers and mothers were not allowed to beat even their children so excessively, and then we asked her how she knew the said boy was not related to the said Deschauffours, answered that the lackey himself had told her that.

11th Witness.

We had approach an individual dressed in brown hazelnut colored cloth, and carrying a bonnet wig, who sad he was named Augustin Caporal, called Languedoc.

SECOND INQUIRY PERFORMED IN 1726

DEPOSITIONS OF FRIDAY APRIL 19

12th Witness.

Michelle Claudine Polet, widow of Jean Barbet, who had been a coachman at the home of Monsieur the Président Le Camus....

Said that master Deschauffours had also stayed on the vieille rue du Temple, at the corner of the rue des Blancs Manteaux, and that there he bore the name of master Des Fourneaux Bellair.

Asked if she knew any details about the said Deschauffours, answered that she knew quite a lot, and that the said Deschauffours, under an officer's name which she had forgotten, had been to a Merchant of golden and silver galloons and bought there twelve hundred livres worth of galloons, in paying for which he pretended to have forgotten his purse and asked the said Merchant to send them to his place, which the said Merchant did, but that the said Deschauffours not being then at home, or rather feigning not to be, and that evening the said Merchant returning to his place, he denied having received anything, and so swore at the Commissioner De Moncrif's.

At which we told the said respondent that we were not asking for an account of the said Deschouffours' swindles, given that we were quite willing to believe he was capable of them, but that we asked her for details related to the crime of which he was accused....

Asked how she knew these details, said that she had them from the above named la grande Jeanne, servant of madame Doreau, from the said Picard, and from Duplan himself.

Asked how the said Duplan could have admitted all these things to her, answered that the said Duplan spoke familiarly to her respondent of all this, that she had done everything she could to get him to marry, or at least take a woman, but that the said Duplan answered that he did not want to get married, and that if he took a Mistress he would have to do as much for her as had been done for him. [!] ....

And the said Picard had added that the said master Deschauffours was a weak and stinking lover, but that nonetheless he was obliged to let him do as he would, given that the said master Deschauffours allowed him to carnally know the young men who frequented his house....

Answered that there was an infinity of people, that she had seen there Monsieur the Count de Katia, etc., the Baron de Troller, a German, and several others....

Answered that she had seen there a young Blond who always wore red heels and who had a very effeminate air... and that he (Picard) had never seen a creature with more beautiful buttocks than the said young man....

Asked if she knew where the said Picard was, answered no, but that she was sure he was no longer involved in this filthy trade, and even that she had been told that the said Picard currently had a mistress, with whom he had children.

Asked if the said Deschauffours had admitted anything to her, answered no, except that he incessantly spoke badly of women.

13th Witness.

Georges Vincent, surgeon, born in Montpellier.

14th Witness.

We had approach an individual dressed in a brown suit with golden buttons and wearing a sword, who said he was named Ambroise Cosme Vitrey.

15th Witness.

We had come an individual wearing a dress of blue damask with white flowers, who said she was named Barbe Chappey, wife of Laurent Le Franc, and that she was from Issouldun in Berry.

To which the said master Deschauffours answered no and that this Monsieur was one of the most skillful men in the world, then the individual dressed in red camlet cried out, at which the individual dressed in drugget said: "Why are you crying out? I am preparing you well and wrapping you so that you will not feel the pain of the incision."

16th Witness.

Laurent Le Franc.

17th Witness.

Pierre Guillois, called Champenois.

18th Witness.

We had come an individual wearing a dress of white cotton who said she was named Marguerite de La Plaine, wife of Pierre Guillois, called Champenois.

19th Witness.

Adrien Boutel, called L'Olive.

20th and last Witness.

Jérôme Jourdain.

Deschauffours confronts his accusers

The *recolement* was a phase in the trial when the witnesses heard their testimony read back and either maintained what they had stated or adjusted or even renounced it. Here it is followed by the confrontation. Given the dark reputation of Old Regime justice since the Revolution, it may surprise modern readers that the defendant had a right to confront his accusers, but the confrontation was also a standard part in the process and one in which the defendant could challenge witnesses directly.

CONFRONTATION AND VERIFICATION OF WITNESSES

In the year seventeen hundred twenty six, today Monday, the thirteenth day of the month of May, nine in the morning, we, René Hérault, called before us the individuals whose names follow and declare:

And firstly Benjamin Deschauffours, supposedly citizen of Paris, accused of having committed and had committed sodomy.

After which, and all the individuals named hereafter being in the presence of the said Deschauffours, we have had read aloud the written record made before us; containing the depositions, testimony, charges and declarations of Jean Petit, called Painque; Regnault Poitret, called Musicien; Arnaud Daniel Perron; Jeanne Elisabeth Cordelier; Thomas Vaupinesque, called Chambery; Marie Le Clerc, the widow Chauveau; Marie Geneviève Anquetil, the widow Finet; Henry Hillaire Finet; David Edouard Taylor; Jeanne Trappel, called Jeanneton; Augustin Caperal, called Languedoc; Michelle Claudine Polet, the widow Barbet; Georges Vincent; Ambroise Cosme Vitrey; Barbe Chappey, wife of Le Franc; Pierre Guillois, called Champenois; Marguerite La Plaine, wife of Guillois; Adrien Boutel, called L'Olive; Jérôme Jourdain ; which witnesses we have confronted and reexamined before the said Benjamin Deschauffours, in the following manner:

Jean Petit, called Painque, declared that he maintained [his testimony].

Armand Daniel Perron, declared that he maintained.

Jeanne Elisabeth Cordelier, called La Grande Jeanne, declared that she maintained, with the reservation that she had deposed that Picard, coming out of the apartment of the said Deschauffours, had said: "They don't need us, because they are all threaded like maybugs!" which the said Cordelier declared to only know by having heard it from La Picarde, and so she does not dare swear to it, and so she retracts having said it.

Thomas Vaupinesque, called Chambery, declared that he maintained.

Marie Le Clerc, veuve Chauveau, declared that she maintained.

Marie Geneviève Anquetil, the widow Finet, declared that she maintained.

Henry Hillaire Finet declared that he maintained.

David Edward Taylor declared that he maintained and that besides he had never seen the said defendant and wished him no harm, having only deposed for the good of his conscience.

Jeanne Trappel, called Jeanneton, declared that she had only heard a part of what she had deposed, and that she had known the rest from master Vincent, the next morning, declaring beside that she maintains her said declaration.

Augustin Caperal, called Languedoc, declared that he maintained.

Michelle Claudine Polet, called La Picarde, the widow Barbet, declared that she maintained.

Georges Vincent declared that he maintained.

Ambroise Cosme Vitrey declared that he maintained, and confessed further that he had had the weakness to not make the said Deschauffours leave at once, for fear of losing the full term of the rent for the apartment occupied by the said Deschauffours.

Barbe Chappey, wife of Le Franc, declared that she maintained.

Laurent Le Franc declared that he maintained, and that he had seen nothing, nor heard, except for a loud noise.

Pierre Guillois, dit Champenois, declared that he maintained.

Marguerite La Plaine, wife of Guillois, declared that she maintained.

Adrien Boutel, called L'Olive, declared that he maintained.

Jérôme Jourdain declared that having questioned the said Grandot, his journeyman, he had not been able to learn any detail regarding the crime of the said Deschauffours, and that finally having pressed the said Grandot, he said that he knew nothing precise, and that everything he had said about it was gossip, for which the said Jourdain, for the good of his conscience, retracts what he said against the said Deschauffours, and does not maintain it at all.

Benjamin Deschauffours declared for his part that he maintained his answers and his denials made in his interrogations, and also in the last answers he made; and then, at the end of some times, the said Benjamin Deschauffours declared in front of the said witnesses, that just then he was so troubled and filled with anger, at hearing so many false accusations that he could not answer us, but that soon he would tell us the truth.

The confession

Three days after the angry words above, Deschauffours gave what appears to be an extensive confession. What is more, for the first time he shows something like compassion, even seeking mercy for others involved.

What happened?

It is striking that no one, here or elsewhere, says that he was tortured. Though this trial was conducted in a non-standard way, it seems overall to have followed the standard judicial forms. Torture just before execution was not an obligatory part of these, but it was quite common, especially in capital cases with numerous others involved. Deschauffours' chastened tone too is quite similar to that of other defendants who had fiercely denied everything, only to become loquacious after having water forced into their stomachs or wedges hammered between boards strapped to their calves.

The best one can do is speculate. It does seem unlikely that such torture, if applied, would not have been noted in the trial record. But if it was not, it is equally problematic to explain Deschauffours' sudden contrition.

The other possibility is that Deschauffours was a devout Catholic and, facing death, sincerely feared for his immortal soul. If this seems extraordinary, consider that in another case a woman who had made what she thought to be a deal with the devil nonetheless seemed at the same time to believe in the God she was offending for Eternity. Such contradictions were not unheard of at the time.

Otherwise, it is striking that 'Duchaufor' (as Ravaisson has it) did not at once kneel for his interrogation. One might expect many defendants to have been recalcitrant in these circumstances, but in fact such hesitation – willful or not – does not appear in other transcripts. It suggests that he was either unusually stubborn or, alternately, only too aware of his situation – enough to muse on it, rather than instantly comply.

The following version is taken from Hernandez. Ravaisson partially reproduces the same statement, but redacts specific mentions of acts and names, and leaves out almost half of it. A few of his changes are noted below to give some idea of what a nineteenth century writer found shocking.

LAST INTERROGATION

of Benjamin Deschauffours

Thursday, May 16, 1726

We had come and appear before us Benjamin Deschauffours, and summoned him for the last time to tell us what he knew of the truth, for the discharge of his conscience, and peace of his soul, the body being nothing, and other exhortations from us to urge him reveal to us all his crimes and accomplices;

The which Benjamin Deschauffours [*Ravaisson has* "Duchaufour"], after having mused some time, finally went to his knees and told us that he was going to at once reveal the truth to us on everything above, at which the said Benjamin Deschauffours told us what follows, and which he assures us is the pure truth.

He declared that truly and maliciously he got Henry Hillaire Finet to come to his place and invited him to eat and had him take opium in his wine, to put him to sleep, during which time Lormay [*Ravaisson says "Lormoy"*], who was the person in clothes of black *ras de Saint-Maure*, had twice known carnally and against Nature the said Finet [*Ravaisson redacts everything after "had"*] and then the individual in clothes of brown silk cloth and whom he does not know having been brought by the said master Lormoy had equally carnally known the said Finet [*Ravaisson again redacts the verb and object here*]. The above mentioned then retired and gave two golden louis to him respondent, who then sent away Finet in the way said in the depositions above and in consequence master Taylor had well and rightly decided that the said Finet's wound was made by rape and carnal knowledge and against Nature.

In regard to the various names of Moulien, Duplessis, of the marquis Préau and de Desfourneau which he had taken at different times and in changing districts, he respondent admitted that it was being known and fearing to be discovered that he hid himself under these different names and appearances.

That the well dressed lord, who, in the presence of J. Petit, called Painque, had said he did not want the boy that he confessed to have offered him, was called the marquis de Merinville [*Ravaisson redacts this name*], and not the marquis of Constantin, as the said Painque had falsely deposed, and that the said young man was named Jean Chanelle, son of a tapestry maker, on the rue Tireboudin, which the said Painque had rightly said, with the exception of the name which he had not known, affirming further that the said Chanelle had never committed the said crime of sodomy [*Ravaisson redacts this*] and that if he had then consented, it was that he needed money to give a Mistress whom he had then, but that had had no effect given the refusal of the said Marquis; for which he protests that the said Chanelle is innocent.

That it is quite true that he took Picard and Lafleur into his service to know them carnally [*Ravaisson, etc.*] but that the said Lafleur never wanted to consent to this, it is why he declares him innocent; regarding Picard, he used him for a long time in this way and even because of that had endured much insolence from him, and on that the testimony of Regnault Poitret was true.

That it is also equally true that he had tried to corrupt Arnauld Daniel Perron, at the request of the Count de Trond, a rich Flemish lord, who having seen him several times at his place fell madly in love with him and who had promised him fifty guineas if he could induce him to come with him to his country, and that he was refused by Perron..

It is equally true that one day he had raped Duplan, son of a tailor, and that the said Picard went to see the said Duplan, who returned to his the defendant's home, and bore the carnal copulation of him and the said Picard, and that finally he delivered Duplan to a Scottish lord for 100 louis, which lord, whose name he denied knowing, had offered a pension of 1000 francs to Duplan and his food for his lifetime.

That the marquis de ...., the count of ...., the marquis Spinelli, the lord of La .... King's secretary, and the chevalier Forbwy, English lord, [*Ravaisson redacts all these names; it is not clear why Hernandez omits some here*] really did not come to his place except for him to produce young men for them and is quite true that he had delivered the young blond with red heels to the said Chevalier Forbwy, and that the said boy was the son of a chandler who lived on the rue Montorgueil.

That he had also delivered a young boy named Bloirau [*Ravaisson: Bloireau*], son of a lawyer, to the said Marquis de Spinelli.

That it was also quite true that he had delivered to the said sir de Monzelli Thomas Vaupinesque, and it was also true that the said Chambery was always taken by force, and had never consented to the said crime, the defendant affirming that besides the deposition by the said Chambery was sincere and true, that the said Chambery was quite a good lad, and that he defendant often felt guilty for having raped the said boy, so that he did not dare greet him when he saw him in the street.

That it is also quite true that he had raped and had raped by three different people on the Rue Montmartre Paul Chauveau, and that he had sold him for thirty-five louis to a Polish lord, who had taken him to his country and that he had never had any news of the said Chauveau.

That besides the story that the said Chauveau had told his mother was very sincere, and that in consequence the said widow Chauveau had rightly deposed, and that the three individuals who as well as him had raped the said Chauveau, two were sons of a coal measurer named Quillain, and the third an Italian named Borghetti.

That the report by Pierre Bomel and David Edward Taylor, surgeons, matched the truth, given that the said Finet had really been raped and known carnally by the said masters de Lormaye [*sic*] and Prezeau, and that he defendant knew well that it was the said Prezeau who had given the Crystalline to the said Finet, given that he often complained of this illness.

That it was quite true that he defendant had kidnapped a young boy of ten to eleven, son of a soapmaker who lived on the rue de Clery, and who was named Le Nain, which boy he had so struck

with his cane that he had broken his head and that then he had
sent him to the hotel Dieu, while the said boy was unconscious
and could not speak, adding the said defendant that he had
threatened to kill the boy if he spoke to the Surgeon, and that he
had kidnapped the boy to please a foreigner whose name he did
not know.

That it was quite true that he had induced Bizetti to get castrated,
although he did not really have any pain, but that it was the
Prince Torelly, an Italian, who had him do that, to take the said
boy with him to Italy, hoping that the said boy would have a
beautiful voice, and would still use him to commit the crime of
sodomy, to which this lord was much given; but that he had been
disappointed in part of his hopes, given that the said Bizetti
turned out to have no voice.

That the individual who had performed the operation on the said
Bizetti was the son of a wigmaker named Gregoire, which
Gregoire had heard the noise of someone coming up, which had
made him flee, adding the said defendant that the said Gregoire
was in no way subject to the crime of sodomy, and that he had
promised him twenty louis for this matter, but that having fled he
had never dared ask him for them.

That everything that he defendant had said in his interrogation
about the intercourse of Picard with the said widow Barbet,
called La Picarde, was quite true, and that the said Picarde was a
thief, and besides the rest of his declaration was true.

That the Baron de Troller, whom she had said came to his place,
in truth only came for sodomy.

That the deposition of Georges Vincent, surgeon, was entirely
true, as well as that of Ambroise Cosme Vitrey, that of Barbe
Chappey, the woman Le Franc and of Laurent Le France, her
husband.

That it was also equally true that he had kidnapped the said
Julien Guillois and had given him to the abbé Cofratti, an Italian,
who often came to the hotel de Bourbon, and who having seen
the said boy had promised and given the said defendant twelve
louis to bring him to him and that he had learned that the said
Guillois had fled and was currently in Lyon, with a wine dealer

who had taken him in by charity, that this wine dealer was named Robert Le Noir, and lived on the rue Mercière in the said city of Lyon, the said defendant begging us, for the discharge of his conscience, to have the above said Guillois and his wife informed of this, since they could be worried about their child.

And that regarding the deposition of Jerome Jourdain, it is quite true that he took at his place and at that of many others drugs for the fundament.

For which crimes, hateful and great, the said Deschauffors declared to us he was contrite and repentant.

The sentence

EXTRACT FROM THE REGISTERS

OF THE SOVEREIGN CHAMBER OF

THE ARSENAL

Given the criminal and extraordinary trial held by us of
Benjamin Deschauffours, a man of low station, accused of the
crime of sodomy and sins against Nature, and in virtue of the
commission assigned to us by his Majesty bearing the order and
commission to judge supremely and without appeal the said
defendant:

Given the verbal trial of inquiry done regarding the said
defendant, the interrogation he has undergone, his answers,
denials and variations, the verification of the said accused and of
the said witnesses, and the confession given by the said
defendant, and all considered:

We have declared the said Benjamin Deschauffours, man of low
quality, good and well convicted of having committed and had
committed the crime of sodomy, crime against Nature, and other
enormous and hateful cases described in the said criminal trial,
we have condemned him to be attached to a stake which will be
set for this purpose in the grève square of this city of Paris and
there burned alive with the minutes of the said trial, on a pyre
which will be lit around the said stake, this done these cinders
thrown to the wind; we declare further all the goods belonging to
the said Deschauffours, confiscated to the profit of his Majesty,
on which nonetheless will first be levied the sum of three
thousand livres of fine to the benefit of the said lord King,
should the confiscation not take place. This was done and
ordered by us, Messire René Herault, Knight Lord of Fontaine
L'Abbé, King's Councilor in all his Councils, ordinary Master of
Requests in his hotel, Lieutenant General of the Police of Paris in
this City Jurisdiction and Viscounty of Paris, only Commissioner
in this part, today Saturday the twenty fifth day of the month of
May seventeen hundred twenty six.

The day and date here contradict most other accounts; Bois Jourdain and others say that Deschauffours was sentenced and executed the day before, on the 24th. The appendix to one period journal gives a slightly different version of the above which ends:

> Judged May 24, 1736. Signed: Pellerin, clerk of the commission.
>
> Executed the said day, May 24, 1726, Friday at eight in the evening.

The same source goes on to say:

> At the bottom of this decision one reads the following details, written in the hand of M. Gueulette [*a substitute for the King's prosecutor, and the collector who had saved this record*]

Some of this concerns others, but it begins as follows:

> He was strangled before being burning, as per the *retentum* of the judgment; nonetheless a man worthy of faith, who was near the pyre, told me that apparently he had not been well strangled, because he had seen him make a rather violent movement at the moment when the fire surrounded him...

This account is unconfirmed however and if Deschauffours was still alive when being burned, it is unlikely that he would have shown it only with a brief movement. When a similar lapse occurred in the English case of Catherine Hayes (described in the Newgate Calendar) "she rent the air with her cries and lamentations".

The note goes on:

> He was not taken to the Grève until eight in the evening, and as there were no honorable amends, he was in a brown suit, like a surtout, head bare, and seemed very repentant; he was a small man, it seemed to me, rather good looking, the face confident enough, and lame by accident, from a fall which had broken his ankle. He had found the secret, before being known for what he was, to gain the esteem of M. Dargouges, civil lieutenant, who

had even named him guardian in trust of mademoiselle de Mortagne, from whom he consumed nearly forty thousand francs in two years. He had a brother-in-law who was a commissioner of war, and who had been attached to the king Stanislas. He had been married twice, was a widower and had a son; it was the parish priest of Saint-Paul who took him to the execution in the tumbrel....

While at the Bastille, he had made a sort of will, written with coal, by which he declared where certain of his things were, and some trial transcripts [?] which were in the hands of the prosecutors. He repeated it and had it read and signed by the parish priest of Saint-Paul, his confessor, and signed after the reading of his judgment.

The confiscation of his goods was given to his son.

Jean Buvat, *Journal de la régence (1715-1723)*, Paris, 1865, II: 500-502

Bois Jourdain says that when the sentence was cried in the street, it scandalized some with its mention of sodomy: "The princesses of Condé asked madame the Duchess their mother what this crime was: 'It is a type of counterfeiting', she told them."

Nattier

The next item Ravaisson offers from this case concerns the tragic case of the painter Jean-Baptiste Nattier (September 27, 1678 - May 23, 1726). He apparently was not so successful as his brother, Jean-Marc Nattier (March 17, 1685 - November 7, 1766), but nonetheless became a member of the Acadèmie Royale de Peinture et de Sculpture in 1712 and still has some reputation today for his history paintings. Mariette said that both brothers were competent and no more (Pierre Jean Mariette, *Abecedario de P. J. Mariette*, Paris, J. B. Dumoulin, 1858, IV:48-51).

While his arrest along with Deschauffours suggests that his actions went beyond simple sex with men, it is also true that he is not mentioned in any of Deschauffours' testimony (though neither are others who follow here). In a 1928 article on his death, Raynaud writes that a note added on Deschauffours' judgment says that he was accused of seducing a very young schoolboy, who was arrested the same time and taken on the same day to the Bastille. But, Raynaud goes on, Nattier was taken there with Charles Lefebvre, who (says the record of his search at entry) carried a tobacco holder, something not often used by children. Raynaud goes on to say (not quite accurately) that children were never put in the Bastille (Ernest Raynaud, "La mort de J. B. Nattier", *Mercure de France*, 26 juillet, 1928, 324-340).

Raynaud also points out that Lefebvre was ultimately released for lack of evidence and deduces from that that Nattier's case would have ended with a similar result. Others however have implied that he was likely to be used, like Deschauffours, as an example.

Whatever the truth, he clearly viewed his situation as hopeless:

NOTE FROM DUVAL

Nattier, painter, entered December 31, 1725, had been locked up in the fifth chamber of the Liberty tower, he had said several times to a subordinate officer of the B., placed with him to watch him, that the affair for which he was arrested was going badly and at certain moments fell into a great sadness; to distract him, he was taken out for air in the courtyard of the castle, and for a walk 4 or 5 times a week. He went for a walk the Friday the day before his death for three hours in the afternoon in the courtyard; having returned around seven, they ate and played a hand of piquet; around 9 or 10 o'clock, Nattier went to bed, talked with him until eleven thirty, he went to bed as well and they then continued to chat intermittently until 2:30. At 7, in waking, he was completely surprised to see blood on the floorboards and near Nattier's bed, he threw himself from his bed and knocked on the door to call the turnkey. Nattier was found dead in his bed and he had cut his throat. Nattier was 40, he was implicated in the matter of the famous Duchaufour.

MAUREPAS TO HÉRAULT

April 27, 1726.

I send you the King's order regarding burial of the body of Nattier who killed himself at the B. I ask you to send me copies of the procedures which you prepared to record the fact and of the writing he did with a pencil which justified him, of which you have taken the originals. (A. N.)

MESNARD TO THE SAME

Versailles, June 11, 1726.

In the procedure of Nattier that I was sent, the copy of this will, which makes up the principal proof to me and which besides deserves to be kept for the cold-blood in which it is expressed, has been forgotten; if you would please have it made and send it to me to attach it, nothing will be missing.

The will seems to have disappeared but the note cited above by the collector Gueulette says that he "left in writing that he had been confessed, had received absolution for his crimes and that to avoid the shame of the execution he had decided to strangle himself, which he did." (The last observation is clearly wrong.)

Bois Jourdain writes: "He used, to accomplish his end, a knife called a *bastille*, made like those glaziers use to put lead on windows, which absolutely does not cut and has a rounded tip."

Mariette says:

> It was one of these bad knives blunted and with no edge, with
> which one opens oysters. He used it to cut his throat, and I leave
> you to guess with what efforts, and what sufferings must have
> accompanied this cruel torture; but he managed it; he was found
> dead in his room, and no more was said of him.

After his death, says Raynaud, the authorities found in his pockets
a small desk key, a toothpick case in gilt silver, two pencil
holders, one in silver, the other in copper, an opera-glass and (!) a
microscope. He had been reading Montaigne's *Essais* (said to be
his favorite) and had written in pencil on the first page: "Of two
evils, one must choose the lesser".

As it happens, he was expelled from the Academy on that
same day. The Academy's decision begins by saying that the
Academy "had been aware, for a considerable time, of the
disordered conduct and the corrupted manners of M. Nattier the
elder" – Raynaud points out sharply that this being so, that august
body had nonetheless said nothing until he had been imprisoned
for four months and it had reason to fear a public judgment.

He was buried, like most people who died in the Bastille, in
the cemetery of St. Paul's:

> April twenty-seventh [1726] died at the Bastille castle Jean-
> Baptiste Natier [*sic*], about forty years old, whose body was
> buried on the twenty-eighth of the same month in the cemetery
> of Saint-Paul, its parish, by us priest signed, in the presence of
> Antoine Roger and of Mre. François André, priest, who have
> signed. Signed: Rogé, André, Chocquet, priest

Anatole de Montaiglon, *Archives de l'art français*, Paris, 1858; IX:92.

Small fry

A few of the accused were treated relatively lightly (being in the hospital was no doubt unpleasant, but certainly not the worst option available to authorities). These are the kind of people who might well have been left alone if not for the repercussions of this particular case. Not all the names are mentioned elsewhere in the available records. (These entries being from Ravaisson the specifics for one case are redacted.)

One item at the start of the file piece reflects the care the authorities took in these cases to spare certain individuals – generally from good families – in these inquiries:

MAUREPAS TO HÉRAULT

May 20, 1726

The King being informed that you are to judge the trial of Duchaufour and of his accomplices next Wednesday, H. M. has ordered me to write you on H. M.'s intention that judgment be withheld on * one of the accused, until an account has been given him of the intervening judgment.

Whether it was Ravaisson or the original clerk who substituted an asterisk for the person involved, plainly powerful people did not want him, or at least his family, compromised.

Others were less important:

REPORT

[July 1726?]

Lefèvre, Dozilis, Gaspard. They were arrested for ..... There was against them a sentence to be held for further investigation, against some during 3 months, and against the others during 6 months.

They can be sent to the hospital, with the exception of Louis, who can be left where he is until the three months he is being held for further investigation have expired, being a young child of 13 or 14 who was seduced and who must be sent to his father who is a farmer or laborer 15 or 20 leagues from Paris.

Annotation. I will speak, on Monday July 29, 1726, to M. the count of Maurepas so that he will send a King's order to transfer from the B. to the hospital, Lefevre, Dozilis and Gaspard, having only sent an order to set them purely and simply free. (B.A.)

MAUREPAS TO HÉRAULT

Versailles, July 28, 1726.

I am sending you the King's order as we agreed together, concerning the lady de Montmorency, the widow Lambert, Le Febvre, Dozilis, Gaspard and Cl. Galland, the execution of which you will, if you please, take in hand. (B.A.)

ROLLAND TO THE SAME

August 15, 1726

You were good enough to promise me the freedom of the little Louis, my servant, the term is expired, I ask you to please give the order for his release.

Annotation of Hérault, August 17, 1726. I ask M. the commissioner Camuset to note if the time of detention for further investigation pronounced against the little Louis has come to an end, in order that I may suggest his liberation.

Annotation of Comuset, August 26, 1726. The sentence of detention for further investigation against Lefebvre, La R. and Masset expired yesterday; it was for 3 months, and that of the little Louis and of Dozilis will not expire until next November 23 being for six months, but I will take the liberty of informing you that it would be dangerous to risk this little Louis in the house of M. Rolland, where he was lost, and the son of whom is a miserable sodomite, and it will be necessary to send him back to his home with his father, forbidding him to return to Paris under penalty of being locked up in the hospital. (B. A.)

MALIVOIRE TO THE SAME

September 6, 1726

The individual whose release is requested by the attached letter is called Ch. Lefèvre. He was arrested as an accomplice of Duchaufour who was burned but his trial having been held by gathering of testimony and confrontations with the witnesses, without there having been sufficient proofs for severe penalties, it was ordered by the judgment handed down last May 25th by M. the lieut. G. of P. that he would be held for further investigation for 3 months, and that during this time he stay in prison.

The term of this judgment expired as of last August 25, without proofs appearing. M. the King's prosecutor gave his conclusions for the final judgment. M. de Monflambert, the commission's rapporteur, having to report the trial next week, it is necessary to order that he be transferred from the hospital where he is, by order of the King, to the prisons of the grand Châtelet, for his judgment. (B.A.)

THÉRU TO DUVAL.

February 2, 1727.

I believe that M. Hérault can grant the lady Mornard the favor she asks for her son, all the more given that none of those arrested with Duchaufour has said anything against him.

[NOTE: 1. He was interned at La Rochelle and the exile order was revoked in 1727.]

Separately, without any other mention of her here, "Duchaufour"'s sister drew official attention:

THE F. DE COUVRIGNY, JESUIT, TO THE SAME.

August 13, 1732.

...I forgot the other day to ask you if you have finally given your orders for the sister of the famous Duchaufour regarding who I took the liberty of presenting you with a memoir. I was told, not too long ago still, that the disorder continued to the great scandal of the whole quarter. (B. A.)

Riotte de la Riotterie

This case illustrates a few points about Old Regime justice in general and about the Bastille in particular. One use of the Bastille was to lock up wayward members of prominent families so that they did not embarrass their relatives. It could also be beneficial for certain people to be sent there when other legal action was being taken against them, since it insulated them from the normal workings of justice.

In the case of Riotte de la Riotterie – who seems to have pushed his luck at every opportunity – both these concerns played a role, along with whatever shame the family felt about his homosexuality. Notably, he had run up debts and, as one official notes, was likely to be locked up again once he left the Bastille. Despite its sulfurous modern reputation, for most inmates, and notably those from good families, as prisons went, it was a far more comfortable option. Bicêtre, on the other hand, was a hellhole. When an official there writes reassuringly that Riotte will be given exercise to help avoid his getting scurvy, it is plain that such concern is exceptional. Common prisoners were left largely to fend for themselves, and it is doubtful that even the most favored prisoners were fed anything like the fine meals recorded at the Bastille.

In *Who's who in gay and lesbian history*, David Parris writes (regarding figures in the Deschauffours case): "The least fortunate was Riotte de la Riotterie, who spent a quarter of a century in prison, largely at the behest of his father, who opposed his release by every possible means." ("Deschauffours, Étienne-Benjamin", Robert Aldrich, Garry Wotherspoon, *Who's who in gay and lesbian history: from antiquity to World War II*, Routledge, 2001), This statement however must be qualified. Riotte's father and later his sister at the least approved of his incarceration, but his arrest in the Deschauffours case was unlikely to have been due to either and the fact that he was rearrested soon after being released five years later seems to have more to do with his own recklessness than any efforts by his family. At several points too he was either completely free or under very light control.

While the father might have had his son locked up merely for being gay, the fact that he felt obliged to protect the family fortune by transferring it to his daughter is also eloquent. The pain he expresses in seeing his hopes for his son dashed seems very real. Also, though it is amusing to read the horrified reactions of some monks and their superior to this whirlwind in their midst, the fact that Riotte continued to blatantly indulge in behavior that was virtually certain to return him to prison suggests something less than a measured regard for his own well-being.

Given his association with Deschauffours, he was probably lucky to not, at the least, have ended up in the hospital. Like many compulsive risk-takers, he seems to have only been emboldened by that close call, and to have acted accordingly going forward.

ANQUETIL TO HÉRAULT.

November 29, 1727.

Samson and de la R. held in the B. have asked to write you. I have the honor of sending their letters attached. Regarding de la R. if M. his father does not see to his clothing needs both in linen and clothes, we cannot avoid giving him this help, as we do for other prisoners.

ORRY TO THE SAME

July 7, 1731.

I have learned that R[iotte de la [Riotterie] the son, has been held at the B. for 5 and a half years. I do not know the reasons for his detention, and should they be of a certain nature, I do not ask you your secret on that, but as it seems to me it can only be in regard to his bad behavior, it seems to me that he has had time to learn to behave. You will do me the pleasure when we see each other to tell me what you think. (B.A.)

HÊRAULT TO ORRY

It is true that R. de la R. is held in the B. by virtue of a King's order of January 17, 1726. The infamies and abominations of his life caused this, and it is saying enough of them to point out to you that he had close relations with Duchaufour, who was burned, and the accomplices of his crimes; since he has been in the B., he has even given signs of his corruption [*supposedly, says Raynaud, trying to seduce his jailers*]. It is true that for about 10 months his conduct has been satisfactory enough, which has prompted me to write his father, grand-bailiff of Melun, to urge him to consent to his release. He asks me by a letter of last June to still hold his son, that his affairs are not in a condition to free him, his creditors pursuing him for a considerable sum and having even attacked the shares; I am then persuaded that if de la R. left the B., he would soon by taken to prison, at the request of his creditors. His father is 84 and it would be hoped for his son that his affairs be in order before the death of his father and that he obtain release.

Nonetheless I have asked for the release order. (B.A.)

One might reasonably think that a long stay in the Bastille would at least initially inspire circumspection when free; apparently not:

LA JANIÈRE TO HÉRAULT.

December 13, 1732.

I have the honor to inform you that it would be very important to send by higher order R. de la R... to his native region since he has left the B., he has always seen suspect people; thus there is every reason to fear from him, above all for the young, what he has been up to for a long time, if order is not imposed.

Within two years, he was back in prison:

August 13, 1734.

Following the King's order which it has pleased you to give dated August 10, 1734, I have arrested and taken to the Châtelet prisons, for disobedience, de la R... (B.A.)

"Disobedience" in this case probably means that he had been ordered to leave Paris – a standard requirement in such cases – and had not done so.

By 1736 he had effectively gone from the frying pan to the fire; i.e., he was now in Bicêtre:

HERAULT TO LEPLAIDEUR, BICÊTRE BURSAR

August 1, 1736.

I ask M. Leplaideur to take the trouble to read the letter of R. de la R. and to note in returning it if his son effectively has received the linen and money which he was to send him, as he writes. I ask him at the same time to note if we can allow this young men the freedom of the courtyard which is pressingly requested for him. (B.A.)

LEPLAIDEUR CIZY TO HÉRAULT.

...It is a man closely linked to Duchauffour. He received the money and the linen otherwise mentioned, that his father had sent him. It is I who had the father hold the receipt from his son; regarding the liberty of the courtyard, I think that it is better that he stays where he is, not only because his father, who is a worthy man and over 90 years old, asks and desires the continuation of his detention, but also because moving him into the courtyards, I could not make him sleep alone in a particular spot, and I would be obliged to have him sleep in a dormitory, several together, where there would be danger, and it would be very bad given the great number of poor people we have here and which grows every day.

Here is what I propose to ease his pains. I will take care to have him often taken out of his cell and to have him put in the enclosed courtyard in the building of *lettres de cachet* where he will take the air, will walk and, in this way, he will be less vulnerable to scurvy. (B.A.)

The "cell" here, by the way, was a *cabanon*. The *cabanons* at Bicêtre have been described as cells that were carefully designed to let in air but no light, but it seems unlikely that an aristocrat's son who had not committed a major crime would have been put in the worst of these. The "building of *lettres de cachet*" suggests that prisoners arrested under one of these "Orders of the King" were kept in a separate building, but the reference is not explained here or elsewhere.

It was the year after this that his father gave a court an idea of the family's distress:

> June 1, 1737 appeared before MM. Godin and de Bissy, notaries at Melun, M. Riotte de la Riotterie, squire, lord of La Riotterie, grand bailiff of Melun and Moret, former governor of the town and castle of the said Melun, "who said that having for a long time reflected on the disorders and dissipations of sir Jacques-François Riotte, his son, who plunged himself into these and to a degree that his father the said lord cannot recall without the sharpest pain." After having taken every care to the upbringing of this son, in the hopes that he would honor his family and be his consolation, he fell into such considerable debauchery and behavior that the King had him locked up in the Bastille, for five years. Fearing that new dissipations by sir Riotte the son do not end up absorbing the remains of his family's fortune, the father gave this to lady Marie-Françoise-Perrette Riotte, his daughter, widow of Pierre Le Comte, when alive squire, counselor-secretary to the King at the Parlement of Dijon, etc.
>
> Côme Lemaire, *Inventaire-sommaire des archives départementales. Seine-et-Marne,* 1875 ;111.

About this time or very soon after, Riotte found himself in easier circumstances, but some distance from Paris and in a monastery; a monastery of hermits, no less. If Riotte was unhappy with this situation, his hosts were even more so:

> BOSSUET, BISHOP OF TROYES, TO MAUREPAS
>
> Paris, January 26, 1741.
>
> The unceasing complaints about de la R. sent to my diocese, in the hermitage of le Hayer, 3 and a half years ago, oblige me to

point out to you the danger there is in leaving him there any longer, and to beg you to give your orders for him to be transferred to some other place where he can be better guarded and more restrained. The hermits of le Hayer, by the location of their house and by their way of life, are not in a state to watch such a man as he must be, and as it seems that the intention of H. M. requires he be. He goes out quite often from the house, and he does not absent himself only to go to neighboring villages, but he comes even into the city of Troyes and he spends rather a long time there, without the monks being able to stop him and the counsel they give him has had no effect.

His conduct, in all the places he goes, and in the very house of le Hayer, is extremely suspect and becomes each day more scandalous.

I would have the honor of going myself to beg you to immediately resolve this, in taking out of my diocese so dangerous a man, if my health allowed me to leave; I flatter myself that you will nonetheless take notice of my immediate prayer.

MARVILLE TO SÉCHELLES

February 15, 1741

I have received complaints from the superior of the hermits of le Hayer against M. de la R., who, by virtue of a King's order which you have asked, after being locked up several times, in Bicêtre as in other houses, because of his disgraceful behavior by which he has long made himself known, having been closely linked to Duchaufour, who was burned for the same crime, and M. the bishop of Troyes, who has received similar sorts, writes to me that it is impossible to keep him any longer in this house, to which he does much wrong by the ill-repute which his corruption, which he continues with young men of the area, has earned him; as it is important that a man of this character be closely locked up and that he not be in reach of frequenting anyone; as it is impossible to avoid it in the place where he is, do you not think it would be appropriate to bring him back to Bicêtre, where, in continuing the pension that he is paid at Hayer, his situation, in regard to support, will be much easier than that of other prisoners; I beg you to write me what you think of this. (B. A.)

SÉCHELLES TO MARVILLE

Valenciennes, February 18, 1741.

I am answering the letter which you did me the honor of writing me regarding de la R., held by order of the King in the house of the hermits of le Hayer; it seems, by his behavior, that he has well deserved the punishment he is experiencing; when I spoke of this to M. Hérault, it was a request that was made to me, without my recalling by whom, but his relations, who so far have paid his pension to the hermits, are known in this, and I do not doubt that they will ask you to lock him up in Bicêtre, as you propose, and I think it is the only thing to do. (B.A.)

THE SAME TO THE SUPERIOR OF THE HERMITS OF LE HAYER.

February 27, 1741.

The count of Maurepas has sent me a letter by which M. the bishop of Troyes asks that you be rid of de la R. before I took any actions in this regard. It is necessary that I know whom to contact so that his pension be continued in the place where he will be transferred. As soon as you have given a positive response to what I am asking you, I will give the necessary orders to have de la R. removed from your place, as you desire. (B.A.)

THE SUPERIOR OF THE ERMITES OF LE HAYER

March 3, 1741

I cannot answer quickly enough to the letter with which Y. E. has honored me. The relief which will come to us from being released from the care of keeping any longer de la R. is so great, that I cannot express it to you. It is the most important service which we can receive of this kind, and it is this which leads me to ask you to give my very humble thanks. The widow L., living at Melun, mother-in-law of the mayor of this town, and sister of de la R. is responsible for the pension, which was first 400 liv,, and which she has raised by 200 liv. She has always taken care to pay the pension every three months. (B.A.)

MADAME R. TO THE SAME

April 1741.

I have received the letter which you have done me the honor of writing me. I am quite sorry that my brother has provided new reasons to complain of his conduct; although his creditors have absorbed all his wealth, I have always carefully paid his pension. It will continue to be paid with the same care in the place where you will judge it appropriate to put him, when you will have informed me that he has arrived there, and whom I must contact to pay his pension. (B.A.)

THE DUKE D'ESTISSAC TO THE SAME

April 28, 1741.

The order which you have been good enough to give to transport de la R. to Bicêtre from le Hayer where he is has not been executed; as this man leads the most scandalous life, and the monks with whom he is staying cannot keep him, their house being open on every side, I beg you to give orders so that the *lettre de cachet* which you have granted regarding this be executed as promptly as possible.

Annotation: Order to put him in Bicêtre at his family's expense for his conduct, and 300 liv. pension.

DE LA VANNEROUX TO LE PAPE

Paris, May 2, 1741.

You did me the honor of telling me, the last time I had that of talking to you, that I would please you by giving notice of execution of the King's order regarding M. de la R. I will tell you then that I arrived the 24th of last month at the convent of the hermits of le Hayer, diocese of Troyes, expecting to find de la R. there, and to transfer him to the castle of Bicêtre, but I was quite surprised when I was told that he was not there, that he had left that morning to go for a walk, and it was not certain that he would return to the house, because apparently he was informed that someone had come for him. I yelled a great deal at the monks of this house, and I held forth to show my rage. Nonetheless the monks were a bit helpful. I was told of two neighboring spots that he frequented; I noted these and went to look for him; finally, after two days of efforts and searching in all the cantons, I found him in the village of Villacerf, 7 leagues from the convent he had left; he had taken refuge with the local parish priest, but having learned that he was being sought, he escaped from this priest's place by a rear door, and went to hide in a peasants' house; I was so informed and there I let him have it, speaking to him face-to-face, he having his sword with him I had him surrender it, and took him to Bicêtre, where he is staying. Think of all the efforts I had to take to succeed in his capture rather than his transport. I am giving you all these details because I have been told that you are acquainted with his sister, who lives in Melun. M. de Marville has told me to write her to ask for payment for this trip; as I do not have the honor of knowing her, I take the liberty of addressing myself to you to ask to speak to her and get her to send me what is due to me for the ordinary and extraordinary expenses that I was obliged to spend in this matter; I cannot get her out of this business for less than 100 liv., unless she prefer that I have my memoir confirmed by a judge, in which case I will do it but if I do that, she will pay the amount of the whole thing, which could be as much as 600 liv., because of the extraordinary efforts I took and which are well documented by good depositions known to M. de Marville. I would be very grateful to you to let me know what this lady tells you, because, should she put up any fuss, I will have my memoir made official by a judge who will make it executable against Mme L.. and that will inevitably cause her expenses, because M. de Marville knows that this lady must pay to M. de la R. the sum of 600 liv. a year for life, and that by an agreement made between them. (B.A.)

BRICHANTEAU TO MARVILLE.

Melun, May 4, 1741.

Although I do not have the honor to be known by you, I flatter myself that my name will be; it is to try to get you to do a favor for Mme L., my hostess for the expenses asked by M. Vanneroux, police officer of the short robe, for having taken her brother to Bicêtre. He is asking 500 liv. and Mme L. is not able to pay them. M. de Sarcé, who will have the honor of giving you my letter, will tell you her sad situation; Mme de Sarcé is her friend, who will join her pleas to that of M. her husband; as for me, I will be quite obliged to you for giving them careful attention. (B.A.)

And so the records for a case that started with a capital trial end with quibbles over a bill – the sort of quibbles which can be found elsewhere in such judicial records.

The parish priest of Saint-Pierre

It is just possible that this was NOT a case of sodomy, since the "monstrous excesses" are never specified; child abuse is another possibility. But this kind of horrified tone is most often used in cases of sodomy.

Note the deference to the Church here, Cardinal Fleury being consulted first.

Whatever his crime, there is something poignant about an ailing priest in the savage society of Bicêtre, pleading to be allowed to walk in the yard.

TAUNIET, *curé*

[entered March 3, left May 30, 1741]

MARVILLE TO FLEURY

M. the chancellor and M. the prosecutor having been informed of the monstrous excesses of Tauniet, parish priest of Saint-Pierre of Saint-Denis, and the horrible conduct mixed with sacrilege which he has maintained until the present, because there was the start of an inquiry in the registry of this abbey, and judging that the scandal in question is among those that is better to hush up by means of authority than to order it punished, following the forms of justice, they have proposed that this bad priest be shut up in a prison from which he cannot communicate.

As Bicêtre is not a secret enough place, it is judged that he must be shut up in the B., and in consequence, His Em. is begged to please approve that an order of the King be sent to arrest him and take there.

Annotation: Good for the B.

VIERNEY TO MARVILLE

...I have just arrested the abbé Tauniet, who is in a carriage at your door. Do me the grace to send to me if you will speak to him, or have me take him to the B. I await monsieur's orders.

Marville notes that he must first consult with Fleury and review the facts. The next note is apparently also from Vierney:

> May 5, 1741
>
> ... Regarding the attached letter which the abbé wrote you, having asked for his belongings, I asked for them from the lady at whose home the abbé had stayed, who told me that the abbé had stayed there for a month, and that he owes 18 livres for rent for his room, as also for the food for all the time he was at her place; that the belongings she had for security did not cover a third of what is required for his payment.

(The reader may have noticed by now that the law's involvement was no impediment to the French love of bargaining.)

"Secret enough" or not, he did indeed end up in Bicêtre, sometime between 1741 and 1744 (the following is undated):

> BONNET, DIRECTOR OF BICÊTRE TO BERRYER
>
> As this priest has been held here for six years, has always behaved very quietly, and is in discomfort, I think one can allow him the freedom to use the courtyard he asks, for which I need a written order, this priest being held by order of the King, accused of horrible conduct, mixed with sacrilege.
>
> Ravaisson, 1737-1748, XV:116-117

He died in December 1750.

Without relations

This case, one of the more well-known of the time, is particularly poignant, since, except for some exceptionally bad luck, these two young men would usually have ended up, like "many people", in Bicêtre. Barbier's period account makes no bones about their lack of connections being one reason they were convenient victims. Note however that, whatever the nominal sentence (and imposing preparations for it), they were effectively strangled, not burned (a mercy which was more and more common by then).

This account includes a rare mention of a sinister figure, dressed in gray, who went before the night watch to spot activities which might otherwise have stopped at the sound of a larger body:

> Today, Monday July 6 [1750], were publicly burnt on the Grève, at five o'clock in the evening, these two workers, that is a carpenter's helper and a pork-butcher, aged eighteen and twenty years old, that the watch found in flagrant délit, one evening, committing the crime of s--- and who apparently had a bit of wine in them to push boldness to this point. I have learned, in this case, that a man dressed in gray walks before the foot squads noticing all that happens in the street, without raising suspicion, and who then has the watch approach. It is thus that our two men have been discovered. As some time has passed since the judgment without its being executed, it was thought that the sentence had been commuted because of the indecency of these sorts of examples which teach to many young people what they do not know; but it is said that a conflict between the lieutenant criminal of Châtelet and the rapporteur [*roughly*, reporter; *a special judge*], as to who would assist at this execution, so much the more since the rapporteur was no longer assigned to criminal cases; but M. the chancellor has decided that the rapporteur would go, even being no longer assigned to criminal matters during the execution. In a word, this execution was carried out to set an example; especially because it is said that this crime has become very common, and that many people are in Bicêtre for this. As these two workers had no relations with people of

distinction, either at Court, nor in town, and they named nobody, this example was made with no consequence for the future.

The fire was made up of seven rows of kindling, of two hundred sticks and of straw, they were attached to two stakes and strangled beforehand, though they were suffocated at once by a sulfur shirt. This judgment was not read out apparently to avoid the name and the qualification of the crime. Reading was done, in 1726, for sir Deschauffour for the crime of s...

Edmond Jean François Barbier, *Chronique de la régence et du règne de Louis XV* (1718-1763): or, Journal de Barbier, July 1750, IV:447

The men's names are given in separate accounts as Bruneau Lenoir and Jean Diot. The sentence was handed down, per different sources, on either June 5 or June 7. (*Encyclopédie méthodique: ou par ordre de matiéres ...,*1787 VII:615)

Tragedy did not impede the period's wit:

July 27, 1750. The parlement of Paris, which rarely makes examples of severity in a certain genre, has had burned, in the last two weeks, two men for the sin of non-conformity and publicly whipped seven or eight women for the contrary sin. These two events gave M. Bertin the idea for an epigram:

"Tell us then, lady Justice,
which of two loves' service do you prefer?
For having lit the torch of Sodom
A poor couple has been grilled on the Grève;
Today, for having sliced some mackerel
and relit the flames that Adam felt for Eve,
On the ass of a donkey we see an honest housewife
For whom, unfairly, you have sought trouble.
Decide nonetheless, because a man must, for God's sake,
be either Villars or Richelieu."

Mémoires secrets, I:451

The Grève was the place of execution; the female form of 'mackerel' was a word for a madam; the Duke of Richelieu was known as a ladies' man and Villars clearly the opposite.

A shining example

The fact that Pascal was broken on the wheel before being burned was clearly a punishment for the attempted murder. It was almost certainly the only reason a (relatively rare) capital sentence was imposed at all.

> By a decision confirming the sentence of the châtelet of París, handed down in the *Chambre des Vacations* of the parlement of Paris, October 10, 1783, des vacations Jacques François Paschal has been convicted of having engaged in the most criminal debauchery towards an errand-boy of fourteen, whom he had lured to his room; and annoyed at his resistance, of having murdered him, in striking him numerous blows with a knife, on the head as on the haunches and in the back, which blows then put and still put the life of the said errand-boy in danger. For reparation of which the said Jacques François Paschal has been condemned to make honorable amends before the principal door of the church of Paris, where he will be taken by the executor of high justice, in a tumbrel, feet bare, head bare and in a smock, holding in his hands a burning torch of two pounds, having a rope around his neck, and a sign before and behind, bearing these words: "*debauchee against Nature and murderer*"; and there, being on his knees, say in a high and intelligible voice, *etc., etc., etc.,* and from there be taken in the same tumbrel to the Grève square, there to have the arms, legs, thighs and kidneys broken alive by the executor of high justice, after to be thrown on a burning pyre and his ashes thrown to the wind...
>
> *Encyclopédie méthodique: ou par ordre de matiéres* ... 1787, VII:615

The decision included a further note that it was to be printed and posted at all the usual crossroads, etc. in Paris and the suburbs. And so, over thirty years after the case of Lenoir and Diot, it was decided once again to advertise what had been hidden in theirs (giving the public the misleading impression that he had been executed for acts "against nature" rather than a vicious attempted murder).

The *Mémoires Secrets* gave this account (note the piquant fact that the police operative here was named Foucault.):

October 13. Since the execution of Deschauffour no sodomist has been executed. The government was afraid to make the sin against nature more common in making it well known. Thus it is that the prince Buaf******, the actor *Monval*, the notary *Margantin* and numerous others taken in the act have only been punished with exile, prison, bicêtre, or a simple punishment by the police according to the personages or the circumstances.

This vice, which was formerly called *the handsome vice*, because it was attributed to great lords, to people of wit or to Adonis', has become so fashionable, that today there is no rank, from dukes to lackeys and the common folk, who is not infected with it. The commissioner *Foucault*, who recently died, was charged with this task, and showed to his friends a fat book in which were written all the names of pederasts known to the police; he claimed that there were almost as many of them as of girls, that is, about forty thousand. There are also public places for prostitution of this sort, and in the Tuileries gardens a canton is known that is affected to catamites seeking their fortune.

Justice thought that it must finally rouse itself about a crime too widespread to fear revealing it and to not demand a shining example. The day before yesterday it had burned a pederast named *Pascal*, who had taken the nickname of *Chabanne*. It seems certain that he was a Capuchin monk, and that he was a priest. He was not given any qualification in the sentence out of regard for the clergy, and further not to draw its complaints.

This wretch first was broken alive, because having encountered resistance on the part of a little Savoyard [*that is, a chimney-sweep*] who did not want to yield to his desires, he riddled him with seventeen knife blows and left him almost dead. This horrible scene took place on the first of October, in broad daylight and in front of almost the whole neighborhood.

Since *Damiens* no execution has been so well-attended, there were people all the way up to the roofs.

Mémoires Secrets, XXIII:204-205

Example? what example?

If Pascal's death was meant to serve as an example, it would seem to have worked as well as chasing the hookers from the Palais Royal (something which was done several times before and after the Revolution):

December 4 [1784]. Pederasty, today the great fashionable vice, like tribadery among women, has been carried for some time to such a degree of scandal at the court, that his majesty wanted action taken against some lords caught in the act. A sort of harem they had established at Versailles is spoken of where the *bardaches* went for their use. It was pointed out to the king that the spectacle of a legal punishment would be very dangerous, would besides dishonor many great houses, finally would no doubt excite more and more the taste for curiosity about this sin. The king as a result of these admonitions contented himself with banishing several. The marquis of Cre***, head of the household of Madame, is cited above all; he was accused of having debauched a *heiduc* of the queen's. Since he has been gone for two months and in his property in Flanders, this rumor is credited to the point that M. d'Angévillier, his friend, has written him that it would be best if he returned to end, in showing himself, the unfortunate rumors being spread about him. Nonetheless he has not yet come.

On this same subject, one of the most famous preachers of Paris, father *Cesaire*, barefoot Carmelite, cousin of father *Elysée*, is cited; it is said that that they wanted to lose him in the Franche-Comté, his homeland, where he is currently, and that he is accused of sodomy before the parlement of this same province. We must await further information on this strange trial.

Mémoires Secrets, XXVII:50-51

TRIBADS

"THE CRIME OF WOMEN WHO CORRUPT each other, is regarded as a type of sodomy." (Jousse, *Traité de la Justice Criminelle* (IV, 122)) The penalties were in theory as severe, though very much (as it was in reality for both genders) a function of circumstances.

Though one (extremely rare) case here shows that the law could take action against women involved with other women, in fact by the end of the century it was talked about so lightly that some – perhaps most – did not even know it *was* a crime:

> Tribadery has always been in fashion among women, like
> pederasty among women; but these vices have never been
> displayed with as much brilliance and scandal as today.
> In regard to the first, since it is not punished by the laws,
> it is less surprising. Thus our prettiest women give
> themselves over to it and make a glory, a trophy of it!

Mémoires Secrets, XXVII:101

This item (from 1786) then goes on to quote a verse explaining that if beauties have become cold in love, it is because "these women do between them.... what is called a courting finger." (The latter expression is a pun, since the standard meaning of doing a *doigt de cour* was to briefly court a woman or flirt with her.)

A note on terminology will be useful to even many modern readers who read French. Quite exceptionally, the satirical writer Brantôme used the word *lesbienne* in the late seventeenth century to refer to women who loved women (Pierre de Bourdeille de Brantôme, *Memoires de Messire Pierre de Bourdeille, Seigneur de Brantôme, contenant les vies de dames galantes de son temps*, 1693, 233). The word also, surprisingly, appears in one of the cases that follows here. But generally in Old Regime France, a lesbian was a person from Lesbos (and so there was no contradiction in speaking of a lesbian man); the term "Sapphic" referred to a poetic meter; when a specific term was used (which was not always the case) for women sexually involved with other women, it was most often "tribad". Or as the Academie Française put it in the 1798 version of its dictionary: "TRIBADE: n.f. Woman who abuses another woman. One avoids this word.".

Like "the handsome vice" it was often associated with the upper classes. A later writer emphasizes this and its apparent absence in the judicial record:

> The little we know of saphisme in the XVIIth century has to do then with the highest reaches of society: the Great Dauphin had a male lover, Adélaïde de Savoie had mistresses. Ladies in waiting who did not yield to the sparkling and irresistible butterflies of the court dying of love for them... were all accused of Greek behavior; the fact seems true enough for several, the princess of Monaco for instance; Christine of Sweden consoled herself in a similar way for the death of Monaldeschi; and Ninon de Lenclos, not wanting to yield in anything to her unsurpassable models of pagan antiquity, seems to have wanted to take for model: "The whole lyre"...
>
> I do not think that any affair of tribadism was brought before the tribunals of the XVIIth century. ...In any case no legal medical expert alludes to a trial of this sort requiring the intervention of an expert; none describes the signs by which one recognizes the habit of *fricarelle*. Further what would they have said, and what precisely has been discovered on this rare question of judicial medicine?
>
> Edmond Locard, *Les crimes de sang et les crimes d'amour au XVIIe*, Paris, 1903, 231.

(The word *fricarelle*, which suggests rubbing or friction, is virtually untranslatable, but should be readily understood in context.)

Less squeamish than the Academy, the chronicles of the time were not shy about referring to known "tribads":

> July 11, 1774. The vice of the *Tribads* is becoming very much in fashion among our misses of the opera: they make no mystery of it at all and treat this peccadillo as a friendly gesture. Miss Arnoux, though having tried her talents in another genre, since she has several children, reversed course, indulges in this pleasure; she had another girl named *Virginie*, whom she used in this way. The latter changed her status and passed to mademoiselle de Raucourt of the Comedie Francaise, who has a strong taste for her sex and renounced the marquis de Bièvre, to indulge it more at her ease. Most recently at the Palais-Royal, at night, sir Ventes, having tweaked miss Virginie on her rupture with miss Arnoux, who is called *Sophie* in these orgies, the latter, witness to these remarks, gave the cavalier an expert slap, which he was obliged to laugh at, asking the kind tribad to excuse him.
>
> *Mémoires secrets*, VII:178

This is only one of many references in the Mémoires, which most often mention Mlle. de Raucourt (Françoise Raucourt, 1756-1815 - Raucoux is an alternate spelling), both in regard to this subject and that of her very admired art:

> September 11, 1779. Mlle. Raucoux's return has been decided. One may recall that the actors did everything they could to oppose her return, and have even deflected the protection of the queen, to whom they stated that the poor conduct and the libertinage of this actress repelled the decency of their body. All these obstacles were lifted by order of the king.
>
> Mlle. Raucoux came to mademoiselle Arnoux's, where she is lodging. She begins today with the role of *Didon*. The whole sect of Tribads is mobilized to ensure her triumph, and the uproar is no less than at her debut.
>
> *Mémoires secrets*, XIV:176

(Her colleagues may have been less understanding, depending on how one understands "poor conduct and libertinage".)

If anything, mentions of Raucourt's inclinations are tinged with affectionate humor:

> The diverse tastes of Mlle. Raucourt are known; they have given rise to the following couplet [*sic*], to the tune of "*On compteroit les diamants*" ["We will count the diamonds", *which may or may not have been apropos*]:

> To celebrate you, beautiful Raucourt,
> Had I not the power
> To change twenty times a day
> Both sex and pleasure?
> Yes, I would be, to express to you
> How dear you are to me,
> A young man to love you
> And a young girl to please you.

> Guillaume Imbert de Boudeaux, *La chronique scandaleuse*, Paris, 1879,116

The verses mentioned above from the 1786 *Mémoires* led to several responses, one supposedly born out of a supper among some women:

> That the tribad *Raucourt*

> Finding a man too heavy,
> Has the orifice
> Of her burning womb
> Rubbed by some feminine finger,

> Is good,

> Very good;

> That does not hurt us at all:
> Me, I think like *Adeline*;

> I like the cock,

> *J'aime la pine.*

(*Pine* still retains the same meaning today; one might guess it to be derived from *épine* (thorn).)

It helped that Raucourt and Sophie Arnoux (Arnould) were both very admired actresses, regarded with something of the indulgence shown to stars today. To the degree that comments about their sexuality were unkind, they tended to be no more so than many remarks made about heterosexuals as well.

In one incident, Raucourt, enamored (like many men) of Mlle. Contat "who played so deliciously in the *Mariage de Figaro*" but without success, discovered that the latter had a large debt and discreetly paid it off. She then went to see her friend, expecting to benefit from her gratitude. But in a quid pro quo straight out of French farce, the latter assumed that one of her male suitors, rejected until then for his lack of generosity, had solved her problem and when Raucourt arrived the door was closed and the man was being rewarded – for *her* generosity. Her rage at the other woman's ingratitude was followed by explanations and general merriment on the part of the public. (*Mémoires secrets,* XXVIII:98-99)

Another reference was slightly crueler, though in truth no crueler than much Old Regime literary criticism. When she wrote a play in 1784, some verse critiquing it ended with these lines (referring to "the author" as "he"):

He is known for his exploits

More than for his work
The work of his fingers
has never earned our vote.

But this newborn,
From a limited talent,

Surprises without touching;

Because the author Raucours

Always labors,
But never gives birth.

Lettres de Julie à Eulalieou Tableau du libertinage de Paris, 1784

And so on... These actresses were not the only ones mentioned, and these are far from the only mentions even of them that refer to their sexuality.

It can be safely assumed that if journalists knew of these women, so did the ubiquitous Paris police. But the word "tribad" is absent from the same sources - such as the archives of the Bastille and d'Argenson's reports - that mention a numerous of male sodomites. So much the better for the women in question, but it makes for a thin historical record; in this case, one assertion in a marital case and only two cases that actually drew official action.

Note that in neither of those two cases was sodomy overtly mentioned. The charges that put the women in prison were more general, to the degree that they were actual charges at all. To prove sodomy – which involved actual sexual behavior – would have required either witnesses to the acts in question or testimony by one of the women involved, neither of which was likely in practice.

An indecent plea

Before there were messy divorces, there were messy separations...

It is not clear here if the simple term "tribad" (so often used by the *Mémoires* itself) was considered indecent or if this lawyer found it useful to enter into excessively explicit detail. Nor, absent other information, can one assume that the challenged court filing was accurate ("indecent" or not).

Roch-Henri Prévost de Saint-Lucien (1730-1808) was a lawyer of some reputation and also left a variety of dramatic and legal writings, including one on "Divorce for incompatibility".

The initial phrasing here is confusing, since it seems clear that Prévost was acting on the husband's behalf. Does it indicate that he wrote a memoir without officially being the man's counsel?

> August 2 [1784]. Me. *Prévost de Saint-Lucien* is a former lawyer much esteemed by his colleagues, but who is said to be difficult, because he is very hot-headed, very passionate; he willingly identifies with his client, and becomes impassioned for his case; which the [concerned] parties regard to the contrary as a rare and excellent quality. This zeal has already led him into several affairs, and here he is now quite recently in the situation of being denounced to his order.
>
> In a memoir that he wrote, because he pleaded not at all in favor of M. du *Villiers*, former musketeer, son-in-law of sir *Bourdes*, the king's dentist, against the wife, who asks for a separation because of abuse and ill treatment; he has not hidden the fact that this lady was a tribad, and he explained himself without mystery; which Saturday led to a hearing by the judges of the great chamber, delivering a judgment which allowed the lady of *Villiers* to enter evidence, to suppress the paragraph of the memoir in which there is question of tribadery, *as contrary to good morals and public decency*. These qualifiers would force the lawyers to expel Me. *Prevost de Saint-Lucien* from the bar. As a result he is busily trying to obtain from the judges that this article of judgment not be maintained.

Mémoires secrets, XXVI:127-128

Madame de Murat

A reader who only knew Madame de Murat from d'Argenson's account might think that her "abominable" involvement with women was the most significant fact of her life. There is not a hint of the writer of children's stories of whom the *Biographie Universelle* says:

> The novels of the countess of Murat placed her in the first ranks
> of this sort of literature.. They are notable for purity of taste,
> wisdom of ideas, the decency of the scenes, and by a touch of
> philosophy which characterized the century in which she wrote
> them. Her verse, of which there is little, is distinguished by its
> facility, and she could have made a name for herself among the
> erotic poets. (XXIX, 566-567?)

Compare this description of her work with d'Argenson's rather different descriptions of the woman herself. A rare example of her verse, however, fits both views equally well, and might be compared to the work of the Greek poet Cavafy:

Pleasure

Must it be so fickle?
I said to sweet pleasure.
You flee us (alas what a pity!),
As soon as we can hold you.

This pleasure, so regrettable,
Responds: Thank the gods;
Had they made me more enduring,
They would have kept me for themselves.

Philippe Gerard Busoni, *Chefs-d'oeuvre poétiques des dames françaises
depuis le treizième siècle jusqu'au dix-neuvième,* Paris, 1841, 100

According to the same article, Henriette-Julie de Castelnau, countess of Murat, was born in Brest in 1670 of distinguished ancestry. She left Brest at 16 to marry (a bit later) Nicolas, the count of Murat, from a very old family:

> Born with much imagination and vivacity, but with an ardent and opinionated character and with too great a leaning towards pleasure, madame de Murat fell sometimes into lapses to which her birth only served to draw greater attention. Suspected of having cooperated in a pamphlet which insulted the whole court of Louis XIV, she was exiled to Loches, by this monarch, at the request of madame de Maintenon.

The article then lists a long list of works she wrote during her confinement (until her release in 1715 by the Regent, at the request of Mme. de Parabere, his mistress).

The two children mentioned by d'Argenson either died or were overlooked by this biographer. "She died... September 24, 1716, leaving no children." Her pregnancy during this same period may indicate that she was, in practice, bisexual, though d'Argenson seems to regard it as one more manipulation.

Her case does not seem to be widely known, but it has been the object of some study. David Michael Robinson's article on "The Abominable Madame de Murat" can be found in *Homosexuality in French History and Culture* (Jeffrey Merrick and Michael Sibalis, 2001). A French scholar says:

> Madame de Murat is, on the model of Charles Perrault, the author of several tales. Married around 15 or 16, she made a name for herself with a political pamphlet against Louis XIV and Madame de Maintenon, which earned her exile, then (in 1702) by "dissolute" conduct, a love of pleasure to the point of scandalizing her contemporaries, she is one of the important storytellers of the Grand Siècle. Her tales mix court life with the marvelous.
>
> *Séminaire du 1er avril 2004 par Séverine Auffret-Musée des Beaux-Arts de Caen - "Liberté des libertines ?"*
> http://perso.orange.fr/michel.onfray/cours_severine_auffret_20041avril.htm (accessed January 14, 2010)

And says Marie-Jo Bonnet:

> Under Louis XIV, there is Madame de Murat, who wrote fairy tales, and who was imprisoned by the king for ten years because at the same time, she loved women, dilapidated the family patrimony, gambled and had dissolute morals.

Interview with Marie-Jo Bonnet, author of "Les relations amoureuses entre les femmes du XVIe au XXe siècle" éditions Odile Jacob, collection « Opus ».

http://www.france.qrd.org/media/revue-h/001/relations_femmes.html
(Accessed January 14, 2010)

For the connection-conscious authorities of the time a key concern was her relation to the wife of the Marshal of Boufflers (which is why the latter is kept informed at one point in Argensons' reports).

> DISORDERS OF MADAME DE MURAT. - September 29, 1698 - I have had madame de Murat warned, as it has pleased you to order me, but, while showing some disposition to change her game, by respect for the King's orders, she seemed resolved to maintain the gatherings at her place, almost every night, with much dissolution and scandal. I hope that a little reflection will make her more circumspect and more submissive; I have taken measures to be informed on this, and I will have the honor to give you an account of the results.
>
> December 6, 1699. - I have the honor of sending you the memoir which it has pleased you to ask of me, concerning madame de Murat; it is not easy to express in detail all the dissolution of her conduct, without offense to decency, and the public is pained to see a woman of this birth in such shameful and such frank dissolution.

Argenson's next report is quite colorful and also gives an amusing picture of the frustrations encountered in trying to gather evidence against the well-connected:

> February 24 1700 [*report written in his own hand*] - Were my zeal completely exhausted, the kind manner with which you have the goodness to awaken it would be capable of giving a new life. I hope, nonetheless, that the details will justify me to you, and that, if I have held off giving you an account of certain matters, you will approve of the reasons which have hampered me.

The crimes imputed to madame de Murat are not of a quality to be easily proved by an inquiry, since it involves domestic impieties and a monstrous attachment to people of her own sex. Nonetheless, I would well like to know how she would respond to the following facts:

A portrait pierced by several thrusts of a knife, by the jealousy of a woman whom she loved and whom she left, a few months ago, to attach herself to madame de Nantiat, another woman of the ultimate dissolution, less known for the fines levied against her because of her gambling, than for her dissolute morals. This woman, staying with her, is the object of her continual adoration, in the presence even of valets and of some lenders on pawn.

The execrable curses spoken while gambling and the filthy talk at the table, of which M. the count de Rousillon, now broken with madame de Murat, has been witness.

Dissolute songs sung during the night and at all hours.

The insolence of pissing out the window, after a long debauchery.

Her audacious conversation with M. the parish priest of Saint-Cosme, as far from shame as from religion.

A chamber maid, let go without having been able to get any of her wages, had promised me she would depose, but the fear that madame de Murat's friends had of that got her paid.

A lackey, covered with a thousand blows and put outside almost in his shirt, used the same method to get justice.

A lender on pawn, to whom was due fifty crowns, saw most of the things I took the liberty to lay out for you: but when I wanted to urge her to sign her declaration, she excused herself in saying she did not know how to write and, leaving my place, she went to threaten madame de Murat that she would depose, in effect, if she was not paid at once; which succeeded.

M. the marquis de Roussillon, to whom all these mysteries of iniquity are known, does not dare reveal them, either by a sort of false honor, or to not recognize his own shame. M. Boistel, councilor in Parlement, the closest neighbor of this house where so many disorders are committed, does not think that it suits his dignity to give me a declaration about them, and he did not even want his lackeys to give me testimony about them.

Finally, M. the parish priest of Saint-Cosme, through whom I have known most of these principal facts, feels that his quality as a pastor is not compatible with that of a denouncer nor of a witness.

I would add that madame de Murat and her accomplices are so feared in the whole area that nobody dares expose themselves to their vengeance.

I can even have the honor to tell you that she is always precisely informed of all the orders which you do me the honor of giving me, so that she is always forewarned against their execution, before I can take any steps to accomplish them.

April 20, 1700. - I have made the intentions of the King known to madame de Murat, and I have used, in this notification, all the care which might ease its bitterness: she has promised to conform to it and has even given me her submission in writing; I have even understood, by her statements, that her plan was to retire to a distant region, at the home of one of her friends, and to completely forget Paris; but she declares that, owing rent to her host and having only for a long time lived off loans, it would be very hard for her to leave without paying anyone, to abandon her son, seven years old, and to not be able to bring him with her, nor confide him to a tutor with board, lacking money to satisfy the one or the other of her expenses: she adds that, not having the least resource on her side, and the fortune of her husband being under seizure, it is absolutely impossible for her to pay the costs of the carriage which would take her to the place of her exile, and that this impossibility (a reason superior to all others) is the only one that has led her to defer her departure, and that she dares offer as an excuse for her delay.

I cannot answer for her interior resolutions, but if her speech was as sincere as her indigence is true, one can count on her repentance and trust in her promises. because she certainly lacks everything, and even the most necessary clothes, most of the furniture at her home belonging to tapestry-makers who would like to have them in their shops and are losing their rent. The wages of the few valets who remain to her are entirely unpaid, and, for a very long time, she has only lived from loans and the little money the cards have earned her.

Under these circumstances, dare I propose to you to stir the King's liberality in favor of a person who has not deserved it by her conduct, but whose present misfortune is not without being worthy of compassion. It seems too that her birth, though a little marred by the conduct of her life, deserves some consideration. and that the King, whose kindness is well above the ordinary, can accord her some help at the same time that he makes her feel the just effects of his indignation.

[December 1701] - I would add, regarding Mme de Murat who is mentioned in this memoir that she has returned to Paris after an absence of eight days, and that she has reconciled with madame de Nantiat, and the horrors and the abominations of their reciprocal friendship cause a righteous horror to all their neighbors.

[PONTCHARTRAIN'S NOTE: Alert the marshal of Boufflers. Arrest madame de Nantiat.]

You have done me the honor of telling me that the intention of the King was that she first be taken to prison, if she resolved to disobey, but I beg you to carefully choose her prison, and to find it proper that I point out to you that this woman, unworthy of her name and of her birth, belongs to people of the first rank, and that she is five months pregnant. I believe than that it would be more just and more appropriate to discuss with her closest relatives the place of her retreat, to have her taken there with some care, and to be that much more circumspect in that all her actions make it plain that she would not be unhappy if her labors were induced.

December 4, 1701. - I take the liberty of sending you a letter which I have received, this morning, concerning the abominable conduct of mesdames de Murat and de Nantiat, which presents, each day, new scenes to the public: the writing of this letter appears constrained, and one can easily suspect that the reconciliation between these two women has excited feelings of jealousy or vengeance in the heart of a third, who previously reigned over that of madame de Murat; but the blasphemies, the obscenities and the drunkenness for which they are reproached is nonetheless real. Thus, I hope that the King would be willing to use his authority to drive them from Paris or even lock them up, if nothing else can be done.

[PONTCHARTRAIN'S NOTE: To order for the one.]

[February 1702?] - Madame de Nantiat has finally left for her own region: thus, I am returning to you the *lettre de cachet* which authorized me to have her taken in the house of the stables of H.R.H. madame the duchess of Orleans, where she was retired.

[PONTCHARTRAIN'S NOTE: Good. Watch.]

Madame de Murat continues to distinguish herself by her outbursts and by the dissolution of her morals. She knows that the King is kept aware of this; but she is counting on no religious community being found bold enough to receive her. I do not, in effect, think there are any, and I could not have a good opinion of those who would be willing to run the risk of it: thus, what other measures can be taken, regarding a woman of this character, than locking her up in a distant castle, where a hundred crowns will be sufficient for her keep and for that of the oldest female servant to be found?

[PONTCHARTRAIN'S NOTE: A. M. de Boufflers]

As she fears that the horror of her life will bring her this order, she claims to be pregnant and adds that her husband not complaining of her conduct, the public is wrong not to approve it: but this poor husband only keeps quiet to not expose himself to the furies of a wife who has thought to kill him two or three times, and the least sober people bear only with pain the abomination of which this woman makes a kind of triumph.

[PONTCHARTRAIN'S NOTE: A. M. de Boufflers.]

April 30, 1702. - I have learned that madame de Murat writes, from the chateau of Loches, not only to her family, but to persons who were the most implicated in her disorderly conduct. It seems then that there would not be less propriety than justice in depriving her of this general liberty, most of her letters only being likely to maintain her lapses and to perpetuate her dishonor. It would be good, too, that while waiting to extract from the debris of her fortune some stipend for upkeep, the commandant be ordered to feed her in the most frugal way. I am willing to believe that he does not allow her to receive any visitors. But it would not hurt if you were willing to write him further, in order that he not interpret your silence favorably and give way to the importunity of this woman who, equally adroit and capricious, will omit nothing to bring him around to her ends.

d'Argenson, 3, 10-13, 17-18, 88-89, 94, 97-98

Listenoy and Lambert

This story – preserved only by fragmentary references in the memoirist and lawyer Mathieu Marais' correspondence with Jean Bouhier, a celebrated magistrate – is exceptional on two counts. For the law to concern itself with a female couple was rare enough (and was prompted here by Listenoy's mother). But more exceptional still, perhaps unique for the period, is the suggestion that the same couple acted as parents – "papa" and "mommy" [*maman*] – to a little girl.

A brief mention in Marais' letter of March 24, 1730 begins the tale, though he refers to an earlier mention by Bouhier:

> Your news of Mme de Listenoy is quite good to know; she
> would have done well to escape as Mlle de Kerbabu did at
> Néaufle. Her affair has been presented: she is waiting for the
> King's prosecutor's conclusions, and then the judgment, and then
> the appeal, and then the decision. All that will take a long time,
> but she is patient and brave.

(It is not clear here if the "affair" here is de Listenoy's or de Kerbabu's; if the former was locked up under a *lettre de cachet*, none of the steps listed would have been necessary. The latter was involved in a different, and celebrated, case.)

In answering from Burgundy on March 21, Bouhier says that she is to be locked up in that region (apparently at Vesoul, per later remarks):

> The great news from here is that any moment the marquise de
> Listenoy is to be brought to our castle sent there by *lettres de*
> *cachet*. It is said that madame her mother has asked for this, to
> stop the course of her loves, whose singularity you no doubt
> know. The letter is addressed to the intendant of Franche-Comté.
> Rumor has it that she has escaped, I will send you the
> continuation of this affair.

His next word was sent on March 28, and seems to be cheering the fugitive on:

> The marquise de Listenoy has in effect escaped and has, it is said, fled to a papal land like d'Assoucy, with the dear object of her mad love. What is good in this, is that she passed through here incognito with no more happening than with the Lambert woman, who is said to be very good-looking, if a little thin. She guaranteed her 6,000 livres for life for her good and agreeable services.

For a magistrate (formerly first president of the Burgundy parlement), he is surprisingly disappointed on April 15, at her getting caught:

> Madame de Listenoy has been silly enough to let herself get arrested at Pont-de-Vaux. She is in our castle and has been given to serve her two ancient witches who are quite likely to cure her of her lesbian [*lesbien*] tastes. Her dear Lambert has been taken to Paris where it is thought she will be locked up in the Saint-Michel convent. It is said that she is very agreeable and that she would a long time ago have liked to have extricate herself from her marquise, drawn in it is said by 6,000 livres income for life. I do not know if it is that which has most embittered madame her mother. She is at liberty to see those who go to see her, but there is not a great crowd; she will find few proselytes here.

But the imprisonment lasted less than a month and on May 12 Marais wrote from Paris, praising Mme de Listenoy's sister, who had gone to Burgundy to have Listenoy released:

> I congratulate you on having Mme de la Vrillière in your Estates. She is a beauty for all countries and all times; she charmed England when she was there; she caused great passions there, and she will always have everywhere the effect which the graces have, Homer had someone who resembled her in mind when he described them. Mme de Listenoy is in Saint-Mandé, near Paris, and it is said that Mlle Lambert's liberty has been restored.
>
> Here is another on them. La Lambert is pregnant, and Mme de Listenoy insists that if she is, it can only be by her; this route to

making babies works in the *pays de Fadeur*. This incident super
or contra-natural will soon have people speaking silliness to
women.

The *pays de Fadeur* is an obscure reference, but a modern
writer says that Marais was hostile towards Lambert and her
(apparently stiff and somewhat pretentious) salon and so called it
"the country of the Bland". (Frédéric Deloffre, *Une Préciosité nouvelle*:
Marivaux et le marivaudage, 1955, reprinted in facsimile 1993, 20)

Housier's response, probably of July 22, expands on this curious
situation and adds the note which makes this case so unique (and
intriguing, since no further information exists on this claim):

I laughed myself silly over la Lambert's pregnancy, and what her
sweetheart said about it. But do you know that while they were at
Vesoul, they had I know not which little girl with them whom
they had taught to say papa to the one and mommy to the other?
Today's pregnancy is then only a second pregnancy.

Marais, IV:116, 128, 147

HETEROSEXUAL SODOMY

FROM A LEGAL POINT OF VIEW THIS, like masturbation, was as criminal as same-sex sodomy. But as a practical matter it seems almost non-existent in the judicial record. This certainly does not mean that it was not practiced. Among other things, using the "rear-Venus" (*arrière-Venus*) was a sure method of contraception at a time when few existed.

Given the paucity of official information on the subject, Brantome's gossipy, if necessarily undocumented, comments may be of interest:

> I have heard of a woman who being madly infatuated with a very decent Gentleman that she had taken as a lover he fearing that the husband do him and her some harm, she consoled him saying: *Don't be afraid because he won't dare do a thing, fearing that I accuse him of wanting to use me by the rear-Venus, for which he could die, should I say the least word, and turn him over to the law. But I keep him so in check and fear, he dares say nothing to me.*

> Certainly, this accusation would have caused no less prejudice to this poor husband, than to his life because Jurists say that Sodomy is punished for the desire: but it is possible that the Lady did not want to tell all, and that he had gone further, without stopping at the desire...

Certainly, I have heard it said that several husbands have been quite infected with such abominations; because wretches that they are and abominable, they make use of their wives more against nature than otherwise, and only use the front to have children; and so treat their beautiful wives, who have all their heat in their fine front parts. Can they be excused, if they make Cuckolds of their husbands, who like their filthy and soiled hind-parts?

How many women of the world are there who, if they were examined by midwives, doctors and expert surgeons, would be found no more virgin by the rear than in front and who would take their husbands to court at once; who hide it, and do not dare to reveal it, for fear of causing scandal to themselves and their husbands? Or is it possible that they take some greater pleasure in it than we might think, for the purpose I have just said; to keep their husbands submissive, that they make love elsewhere...

Summa Benedicti says, that if the husband wants to know her part [*sic*]so against the natural order, he sins mortally and if he claims that he can use his wife as he will, he falls into the hateful and nasty heresy of some Jews and bad Rabbis...

And if the man so wants to cause his wife's loss, she is allowed to separate from him; nonetheless, he says, those who love God must never consent, rather cry out they are being forced, despite the scandal this might cause, and the dishonor, nor the fear of death; because it is better to die, says the law, than consent to the harm.

He then adds, with some shock, that the same work allows any form of congress which can lead to pregnancy, then goes on to say this might make sense when a woman has terrible breath, for instance. "In that case, what can a husband or a lover do, if he does not resort to some extravagant position; but above all let him not go to the rear-Venus."

Should a wife in fact have wanted to brave public embarrassment and accuse her husband of this "unnatural" act, it is not at all clear that she would have been successful. An extremely rare example of this came in what would be a divorce case today, but was limited to a separation at the time, and even then hard to obtain. In his article on that subject, the jurist Denisart mentions "the lady ***" who, in seeking a separation:

> Offered to prove that her husband wanted to force her to commit a crime quite opposed to women's leanings. It was a fact articulated as a cause of appeal, which was pleaded in a closed session. The public minister taking the floor deposed a complaint, and asked that the fact be investigated: but it was rejected as seeming improbable.

A decision of February 1745 refused her the separation and ordered her to a convent for a year. (Denisart, *Collection de décisions nouvelles et de notions relatives à la jurisprudence actuelle*, Paris, 1777, IV:369.)

The de facto existence of this largely unacknowledged practice gave rise to one of the more memorable ribald quips from the period. The notoriously bisexual Sophie Arnould had an Italian friend whose tastes were said to be "diverse" in a different way. When this woman wondered at one of their friends' always getting pregnant so easily, Arnould said, "That's easy for you to say; [but] a mouse with only one hole is soon taken." (« *Vous en parlez bien à votre aise, ...une souris qui n'a qu'un trou est bientôt prise.* ») (*Mémoires secrets*, June 2, 1763)

The writer by the way says that he doubted Arnould "had the gloves" for this remark; that is, that she was the first to say it. This was a reference to an old custom of giving a pair of gloves to the messenger who was first to bring a piece of news. (Henri Bué, *First steps in French idioms*, Paris, 1910)

SODOMITE ARGOT

ANY GROUP FORCED TO LIVE in secrecy will develop an alternate language. In the case of the "sodomites" of earlier centuries, such language was augmented by not only by an imposed association with the prison system (however imperfectly acknowledged itself by officialdom), but by the use career criminals made of that group's vulnerability.

Which is to say, more briefly, that a rich "argot" existed around homosexuality, certainly in the nineteenth century (when such language was first cataloged), but very probably before. The master criminal/spy/police chief Vidocq was one of the first to record argot in general, in *Thieves: Physiology of their morals and their language*, dated 1837. Some of the terms he mentions still exist today, with at least similar meanings:

- By this period, *bougre*, the word which gave English speakers "bugger", had become so generic an insult its original meaning was rarely intended, if never quite forgotten. Its own origin might surprise some: it was derived from *Bulgare* - that is, Bulgarian. Bearing in mind that the French word appears to have referred to a specific group of Bulgarians:

    Heretics and in particular... Cathars, also called Cotereaux, Rupterians, Poplicans, Bonshomes [*goodfellows*], Bégars, Patarins, etc.... It is not impossible, says Baissac, in his *Histoire de Diable et de la diablerie francaise*, that the idea of sodomy attached to this word was suggested by the point in their doctrine which, proscribing marriage as a sacrament and only admitting it as a bad inevitability from which the perfect among them freed themselves, would seem to favor the foul life for which sodomites were reproached. Public opinion, in the middle ages, was ready enough to make sodomy a corollary of celibacy.

l'Intermediaire des Chercheurs, 1895-2 (62)

- *Tante* ("aunt") - "man who has a woman's tastes, the woman of men's prisons". Today: "queen" (in the slang sense). Vidocq accompanies this item with a long discourse on homosexuality in prison, which includes the following remark about "former times":

  In the jails and the prisons, one often sees with no pain audacious thieves attach themselves to young pederasts, because then they no longer think about escaping; the directors and guards of the penitentiary have even sometimes allowed these *marriages* to be celebrated with a certain ceremony; these abuses no longer exist, it is true, people hide today what in other times was done openly, but the evil still exists.

  (163)

- *Pédé* – that is, "pédéraste". Today: same, if somewhat less condemning.

- *Chanteur* ("singer") - blackmailer. Today: same meaning for "master singer" (*maitre chanteur*)

The fact that these terms have lasted almost 200 years suggests that others noted by Vidocq may already have been in use under the Old Regime. Here are some of these:

- *Rivette* - Young sodomite (also prostitute, in the provinces) (65)

- *Tinteur* - Young sodomite (167)

Several terms were used in jail for the same concept: *Corvette* (89), *Frigate* (179), *Galine* (183).

Lorédan Larchey's *Dictionnaire Historique d'Argot* (1888) offers a number of others, though rather prudishly groups them under the verb "to be" ("Etre"), explaining that one can be "of" the following (most of which are not defined in any corresponding entry): "*bicque*" and "*bouc*", "*coquine*" [*which more often means cute or flirtatious today*], "*pédéro*", "*tapette*', "*persilleuse*", "*honteuse*" [shameful], "*gosselin*", "*emproseur*", "*émile*", "*gousse*", "*gougnotte*", "*chipette*", "*magnusse*", etc.

Some of these terms have alternate meanings in other sources.

Vidocq also mentions this term:

> *Jesus* - Male prostitutes also trained to steal; their specialty was to lead men into situations ripe for blackmail
> (235)

And provides elsewhere an explanation of the role they played, a role that undoubtedly existed in the past and certainly exists today (gay tourists in Beijing, for instance, have been subject to a similar scam):

> The Blackmailers [*Chanteurs*] have at their disposition young men endowed with a pretty physiognomy, who go circle about such and such financier, such and such noble individual, and even some magistrate who only remembers from his classics studies the odes of Anacreon to Bathylle, and the passages of the Bucolics of Virgil addressed to Alexis; if the *mark* [*pantre*] takes the bait, the *Jesus* takes him to a convenient place, and when the crime is made plain, sometimes even when it has already begun to be executed, a police agent arrives of a respectable size and corpulence: "Ah! I've got you," he says; "follow me to the police commissioner." The *Jesus* cries, the sinner begs; tears and prayers are useless. The sinner offers money, the fake town sergeant is incorruptible, but the supposed commissioner of police is not implacable; everything works out, finances permitting, and the statement is thrown in the fire.

It is not always this way that the Blackmailers proceed, it is sometimes the brother of the young man who replaces the town sergeant, and his father who plays the role of the police commissioner; this last way of proceeding is even the most used.

Many people, even certain that they have to do with hustlers, have nonetheless paid; if they had protested, the *Blackmailers*, it is true, would have been punished, but the turpitude of the complainants would have been known; they kept their mouths shut and did well.
(63-64)

Vidocq's comments on gay cruising areas may also have been valid for earlier times, though the "house" he names was likely to be of more recent date (those specializing in this research may care to track this reference further):

The *Couch [Canapé]* is the normal meeting place of pederasts; the Queens meet there to give these blasé libertines, who almost all belong to the eminent classes of society, the objects they desire; the quais, from the Louvre until the Pont-Royal, the rue Saint-Fiacre, the boulevard between the rue Neuve de Luxembourg and the rue Duphot, are very dangerous *Couches*. It is understandable, up to a point, that police surveillance of these places is imperfect; but what is incomprehensible, is that the existence of certain houses, entirely dedicated to the descendants of the Gomorrans, be tolerated; among these houses, I must indicate that named [*nommé*; masculine], or rather (to keep for this amphibian being the qualification he [*il*] or she [*elle*] gives itself) that named [*nommée*; feminine] Cottin, rue de Grenelle Saint-Honore, No 3; the police have already several times had closed this house, filthy receptacle of all that Paris holds of muck, and it always reopened.
(54-55)

PRINCIPAL WORKS CITED

Archives de la Bastille; collected and edited by François Ravaisson Mollien A. Durand et Pedone-Lauriel, Paris, 1866-1904

Ravaisson produced his 19 volume collection of the Bastille archives from what could be found of these after the Revolution. Despite the many missing files, some errors in transcription and puritanical redacting, the collection provides a rich and revealing look at life inside and often outside the Bastille.

D'Argenson, René. *Rapports inédits du lieutenant de police René d'Argenson, 1697-1715;* introduction and notes by Paul Cottin, Paris 1891.

D'Argenson's reports (mainly to the Secretary of State) as head of the Paris Police appear in several collections, including the Bastille archives. They have a very personal tone, indignant or compassionate depending on the case.

Bachaumont, L. Petit de, M.-F. Pidansat de Mairobert and Moufle d'Angerville, *Mémoires secrets pour servir à l'histoire de la République des Lettres en France, depuis MDCCLXII, ou Journal d'un observateur, contenant les analyses des pièces de théâtre qui ont paru durant cet intervalle, les relations des assemblée littéraires...* Chez John Adamson, London, 1783-1789

This periodical, founded by Bachaumont, was continued by others after his death, and is one of the principal contemporary sources on 18th century France.

Barbier, Edmond Jean François, *Chronique de la régence et du règne de Louis XV* (1718-1763): or, Journal de Barbier, G. Charpentier et cie, Paris, 1885

A journal which is another major contemporary source for this period.

Hernandez, Dr Ludovico, *Les Procès de Sodomie aux XVIe, XVIIe et XVIIIe siècles. Publiés d'après les documents judiciaires conservés à la Bibliothèque nationale*; Bibliothèque des Curieux, Paris, 1920

Written under a pseudonym by Louis Perceau and Fernand Fleuret, this collection of sodomy trials from previous centuries is one of the rare sources to include nearly complete transcriptions of several famous trials.

Marais, Matthieu, *Journal et mémoires de Mathieu Marais ...: sur la régence et le règne de Louis XV (1715-1737)*, Firmin Didot frères, Paris, 1864

Colorful memoirs and correspondence from a period lawyer. He tends to touch on everything quickly, whatever its relative importance, but is a valuable source on a number of incidents and cases.

www.ingramcontent.com/pod-product-compliance
Lightning Source LLC
Chambersburg PA
CBHW060618290526

45793CB00001B/69